Federal Aviation Administration (FAA) Reauthorization: An Overview of Legislative Action in the 111th Congress

Bart Elias, Coordinator
Specialist in Aviation Policy

October 8, 2009

Congressional Research Service

7-5700

www.crs.gov

R40410

CRS Report for Congress

Prepared for Members and Committees of Congress

Summary

Funding authorization for aviation programs set forth in Vision 100—Century of Aviation Reauthorization Act (P.L. 108-176) and authorization for taxes and fees that provide revenue for the aviation trust fund expired at the end of FY2007. While Federal Aviation Administration (FAA) reauthorization legislation was considered during the 110th Congress, the only related legislation enacted consisted of several short-term extensions for aviation trust fund revenue collections and aviation program authority. The Federal Aviation Administration Extension Act, Part II (P.L. 110-330) extended these authorizations until March 31, 2009, thus carrying the issue of FAA reauthorization over to the 111th Congress. On March 30, 2009, the Federal Aviation Administration Extension Act of 2009 (P.L. 111-12) was enacted, further extending revenue collections and aviation program authority through the end of FY2009, and on October 1, 2009, the Fiscal Year 2010 Federal Aviation Administration Extension Act (P.L. 111-69) was enacted, further extending this authority through the end of calendar year 2009.

On February 11, 2009, Representative Oberstar introduced the FAA Reauthorization Act of 2009 (H.R. 915). The bill is similar to FAA reauthorization legislation passed by the House during the 110th Congress (see H.R. 2881, 110th Congress). H.R. 915, as amended was passed by the House on May 21, 2009. H.R. 915 would authorize almost $54 billion for FAA programs over three years spanning from FY2010 through FY2012. The financing title of the bill would raise fuel taxes for corporate jets and other general aviation aircraft, but would keep fuel taxes paid by the airlines and passengers' taxes at their current rates. The bill would also allow airports to increase passenger facility charges (PFCs), raising the maximum from $4.50 to $7 per passenger. The bill would increase authorized spending for facilities and equipment to support development of Next Generation (NextGen) air traffic modernization initiatives, and would authorize increased funding for airport infrastructure improvement grants. The bill seeks modifications in FAA management and oversight of NextGen air traffic modernization projects, and includes provisions addressing system capacity, aviation safety, environmental issues, and airline industry issues, including airline passenger rights issues.

On July 14, 2009, Senator Rockefeller introduced the FAA Air Transportation Modernization and Safety Improvement Act (S. 1451), containing a two-year FAA reauthorization proposal. A markup session was held by the Senate Committee on Commerce, Science, and Transportation on July 21, 2009, and the bill, as amended, was ordered reported. S. 1451 would authorize $34.56 billion over a two-year span covering FY2010 and FY2011. Unlike the Aviation Investment and Modernization Act of 2007 (S. 1300, 110th Congress), S. 1451 does not contain any proposal for aviation system user fees. Rather, it focuses on accelerating the deployment of NextGen air traffic technologies and a number of safety issues, including the safety of air ambulance operations, unmanned aircraft, commuter airlines, and FAA oversight of airlines and aircraft repair stations. The bill seeks to streamline the PFC approval process, but does not seek any increase to maximum PFC levels. The bill also seeks to improve airline consumer service through enhanced disclosure requirements and contingencies for flights that are substantially delayed, and it seeks an increase in funding for Essential Air Service (EAS) subsidies and small community air service grants.

This report will be updated as needed.

Contents

Tables

Contacts

Background

Funding authorization for aviation programs set forth in Vision 100—Century of Aviation Reauthorization Act (P.L. 108-176, hereinafter referred to as "Vision 100") expired at the end of FY2007. Federal Aviation Administration (FAA) reauthorization legislation was considered at length during the 110th Congress. During the first session of the 110th Congress, the House passed the FAA Reauthorization Act of 2007 (H.R. 2881, 110th Congress). A Senate bill (S. 1300, 110th Congress) was ordered reported, as was a transportation infrastructure financing bill (S. 2345, 110th Congress) containing provisions for modifying and reauthorizing the existing tax and fee structure for aviation. In early May 2008, the Senate attempted, but failed, to take up consideration of H.R. 2881, a reflection of disagreements regarding direct user fee proposals in S. 1300 and various labor provisions in the bills.

Without passage of FAA reauthorization legislation, aviation trust fund revenue collections and aviation program authority have been continued through a series of short term extensions passed by the 110th Congress. The Federal Aviation Administration Extension Act, Part II (P.L. 110-330) extended these authorizations until March 31, 2009, thus carrying the issue of FAA reauthorization over to the 111th Congress. On March 30, 2009, the Federal Aviation Administration Extension Act of 2009 (P.L. 111-12) was enacted, further extending revenue collections and aviation program authority through the end of FY2009, and on October 1, 2009, the Fiscal Year 2010 Federal Aviation Administration Extension Act (P.L. 111-69) was enacted, further extending this authority through the end of calendar year 2009.

This report tracks the status of ongoing legislative action and debate related to FAA reauthorization. It is organized into six major program areas: aviation system finance; airport financing; FAA management and organizational issues; system capacity and safety; environmental issues; and airline industry issues. In several cases, provisions that appear in various unrelated sections of proposed legislation have been rearranged in this report in an effort to group and discuss related items in an issue-driven or programmatic context. Since this report is primarily written as a means of communicating key legislative provisions under consideration in the ongoing FAA reauthorization process, it does not go into detail regarding the specific policy issues behind these legislative proposals.

Legislative Status

On February 9, 2009, Representative Oberstar introduced the FAA Reauthorization Act of 2009 (H.R. 915). The bill is similar in many respects to the FAA Reauthorization Act of 2007 (H.R. 2881, 110th Congress), which was passed by the House during the 110th Congress. In comparison, H.R. 915 specifies slightly higher annual funding authorization levels, and would authorize FAA programs over a three-year span from FY2010 through FY2012, instead of a four-year authorization covering FY2008 through FY2011.

On March 5, 2009, the House Committee on Transportation and Infrastructure ordered H.R. 915 reported with the addition of a "manager's amendment" that was offered by Representative Oberstar and agreed to by a voice vote of the full committee. It was reported on March 19, 2009 (H.Rept. 111-119).

On March 30, 2009, the Federal Aviation Administration Extension Act of 2009 (P.L. 111-12) was enacted, extending authorization of aviation programs and revenue collections through the end of FY2009. The act authorizes a total of $15,856 million for FAA programs in FY2009. It also extends authority to collect aviation taxes and fees at existing rates.

H.R. 915 was brought before the House on May 21, 2009, and passed by a vote of 277-136. Like H.R. 2881 (110th Congress), House-passed H.R. 915 includes a trust fund financing title that would increase aviation fuel taxes for non-commercial operators, but does not include any direct user fee funding mechanisms as proposed by the FAA under the Bush Administration, or any surcharge or direct user fee proposal such as the one included in the Senate bill during the 110th Congress (S. 1300, 110th Congress).

On July 14, 2009, S. 1451, the FAA Air Transportation Modernization and Safety Improvement Act, a two-year FAA reauthorization bill, was introduced by Senator Rockefeller. Unlike the Aviation Investment and Modernization Act of 2007 (S. 1300, 110th Congress), S. 1451 does not contain any proposal for aviation system user fees. Rather, it focuses on accelerating the deployment of NextGen technologies and a number of safety issues, including the safety of air ambulance operations, unmanned aircraft, commuter airlines, and FAA oversight of airlines and aircraft repair stations.

On July 21, 2009, the Senate Committee on Commerce, Science, and Transportation convened a markup session on S. 1451 and ordered the bill to be reported favorably with the inclusion of a number of amendments agreed to by the committee.

On October 1, 2009, President Obama signed the Fiscal Year 2010 Federal Aviation Administration Extension Act (P.L. 111-69). The act authorizes aviation trust fund revenue collections and expenditure authority, Airport Improvement Program (AIP) grant authority, and authority for FAA programs for a three month period, up until the end of calendar year 2009. AIP obligation authority was extended through FY2010 under the act.

Proposed Funding Authorization Levels

Funding authorization levels for the FAA have been historically split among four principal accounts: Operations and Maintenance (O&M); the Airport Improvement Program (AIP) or Grants in Aid for Airports; Facilities and Equipment (F&E); and Research, Engineering, and Development (RE&D). The FAA, under the Bush Administration, had proposed a restructuring of these accounts, largely to separate operational activities carried out by the Air Traffic Organization (ATO) from FAA's regulatory functions. However, Congress has not gone along with these proposed modifications in either appropriations or reauthorization legislation.

H.R. 915

H.R. 915 would authorize almost $54 billion for FAA programs over three years spanning from FY2010 through FY2012. Proposed authorization levels specified in the bill are presented in **Table 1**. The bill would increase authorized spending for O&M, F&E, and R,E & D functions to support development of the Next Generation Air Transportation System (NGATS or NextGen) air traffic modernization initiatives, and would authorize increased funding for airport infrastructure improvement grants under the Airport Improvement Program (AIP). Overall annual increases to aggregate funding authorization average between roughly 3.5% and 4.0% over the authorization period. H.R. 915 proposes considerable increases to the F&E account. These increases are largely being driven by an emphasis on accelerating NextGen modernization efforts.

S. 1451

S. 1451 would authorize almost $35 billion for FAA programs for FY2010 and FY2011. Proposed authorization levels, presented in **Table 1**, roughly match amounts specified in H.R. 915, with the Senate bill providing slightly lower amounts for O&M and slightly higher amounts for F&E, reflecting its emphasis on accelerating the development and deployment of NextGen technologies and flight procedures to exploit those technologies. Amounts for AIP specified in S. 1451 are identical to the amounts specified in H.R. 915, while amounts for RE&D functions are slightly lower, but, nonetheless, are considerably higher than historical appropriations amounts.

Using RE&D funding, the bill seeks to establish a research grant program for undergraduate students and students at technical colleges examining training requirements for aircraft maintenance and the impact of new technologies on training requirements for pilots and air traffic controllers.

Table 1. Proposed Reauthorization Funding Levels for FAA Accounts

($ in millions)

Account	FY2010	FY2011	FY2012
FAA Operations and Maintenance (O&M)			
House-passed (H.R. 915)	9,531	9,936	10,350
Senate	9,336	9,620	-
Conference	-	-	-
Enacted	-	-	-
Airport Improvement Program (AIP)			
House-passed (H.R. 915)	4,000	4,100	4,200
Senate	4,000	4,100	-
Conference	-	-	-
Enacted	-	-	-
Facilities and Equipment (F&E)			
House-passed (H.R. 915)	3,259	3,353	3,506
Senate	3,500	3,600	-
Conference	-	-	-
Enacted	-	-	-
Research, Engineering, and Development (RE&D)			
House-passed (H.R. 915)	215	226	245
Senate	200	206	-
Conference	-	-	-
Enacted	-	-	-
Totals			
House (H.R. 915)	17,005	17,615	19,301
Senate	17,036	17,526	-
Conference	-	-	-
Enacted	-	-	-

Source: CRS analysis of H.R. 915 and S. 1451.

Aviation System Finance

Since passage of Vision 100, there has been considerable discussion about the long-term health of the existing trust-fund-based FAA financing system. There are many who believe that the existing system will have difficulty providing all of the funding that the agency will need in the years ahead. **Table 2** shows the existing aviation trust fund revenue structure.

In the 110th Congress, the Bush Administration suggested that a new funding system, based on user fees that were more closely tied to aviation industry flight activity, should be adopted. Congress, and many, but not all, aviation groups chose to basically ignore the Bush

Administration proposals. Legislation passed by the House and considered in the Senate during the 110th Congress appears to have been largely influenced by aviation interests, especially those representing the general aviation (GA) portion of the industry who asserted that the existing funding system could be tweaked in such a way that it would remain adequate at least until the next reauthorization cycle.

Table 2. Aviation Taxes and Fees

Tax or Fee	Existing Tax or Fee Rate (2009)	H.R. 915	Senate
Passenger Ticket Tax (domestic)	7.5%	NA	NA
Flight Segment Tax (domestic)	$3.60	NA	NA
Cargo Waybill Tax	6.25%	NA	NA
Frequent Flyer Tax	7.5%	NA	NA
General Aviation Gasoline[a]	19.3 cents/gallon	24.1 cents/gallon	NA
General Aviation Jet Fuel (Kerosene)[a]	21.8 cents/gallon	35.9 cents/gallon	NA
Commercial Jet Fuel (Kerosene)[a]	4.3 cents/gallon	NA	NA
International Departure/Arrivals Tax (indexed to CPI) (prorated Alaska/Hawaii from mainland)	$16.10 (Alaska/Hawaii to mainland - $8)	NA	NA

Source: Compiled by CRS from existing statutes and proposed legislation.

a. Does not include 0.1 cents/gallon for the Leaking Underground Storage Tank (LUST) trust fund.

H.R. 915

The House Committee on Transportation and Infrastructure (T&I) does not have jurisdiction over the aviation taxes and fees that constitute the revenue stream for the airport and airway trust fund (aviation trust fund). The Committee on Ways and Means, which has jurisdiction on revenue issues, held a Hearing on the Financial Status of the Airport and Airway Trust Fund on May 7, 2009. As had been the case in the 110th Congress, the T&I Committee recommended a modest increase in the general aviation gasoline tax to 24.1 cents per gallon and in the general aviation jet fuel tax to 35.9 cents per gallon, which the Ways and Means Committee chose to support. The Ways and Means Committee did not mark up separate legislation on this issue. Rather, the Committee provided a Revenue Title, including the proposed fuel tax changes, which was incorporated into H.R. 915 as an amendment during floor consideration of the bill.

As passed by the House, H.R. 915 also includes a provision calling for the adjustment of existing overflight fees (flights that do not take off or land in the U.S.) (these fees are currently used primarily to fund a portion of the Essential Air Service (EAS) program). The FAA is to adjust these fees by expedited rulemaking to insure that the fees are reasonably related to the cost of providing air traffic services for overflights. The bill, however, specifically excludes altitude as a factor that can be used in the adjustment of the overflight fees.

Registration, Certification, and Related Fees

The bill includes fees for aircraft registration, airman certificates, and other types of FAA-provided documentation. It also provides that these fees may be adjusted over time if the FAA's cost accounting system indicates that the cost of providing these services to the aviation sector are higher/lower than the fee levels established in the bill.

S. 1451

The bill reported by the Senate Committee on Commerce, Science, and Transportation does not include any finance provisions. Jurisdiction over these issues in the Senate lies with the Senate Committee on Finance. Finance has not yet considered a revenue title for the bill, but is likely to do so before Senate floor consideration of the bill.

Airport Financing

The Airport Improvement Program (AIP) provides federal grants for airport development and planning. AIP funding is usually limited to capital improvements related to aircraft operations. Commercial revenue-producing portions of airports and airport terminals are improvements that are generally not eligible for AIP funding. AIP money cannot usually be used for airport operational expenses or bond repayments. AIP funds are distributed either as formula grants or as discretionary grants. Small airports are much more dependent on AIP grants than large and medium hub airports. The larger airports can more easily generate revenue from user fees and have historically had the financial wherewithal to successfully access the bond market. For background and legislative history of federal aid to airports, including a description of the AIP program, as well as an overall discussion of AIP issues, see CRS Report R40608, *Airport Improvement Program (AIP): Reauthorization Issues for Congress*, by Robert S. Kirk.

The Passenger Facility Charge (PFC) program provides a source of non-federal funds intended to complement AIP spending. The PFC is a local tax imposed, with federal approval, by an airport on each boarding passenger. PFC funds can be used for a broader range of projects than AIP grants and are more likely to be used for "ground side" projects. PFCs can also be used for bond repayments.

The AIP and PFC programs are the sources of funds for airport capital development that have the most federal involvement. Other sources are bonds, state and local grants, and airport revenue.

H.R. 915 as passed and S. 1451 as reported by the Senate Committee on Commerce, Science, and Transportation retain the basic AIP program size, structure, and funding distribution. The bills would increase the program's overall year-over-year authorization level by $100 million for each of the years covered by the bills. As a three-year bill, H.R. 915 would fund AIP for FY2010 through FY2012, whereas S. 1451 would only fund the program for two years, FY2010 and FY2011.

H.R. 915 would raise the PFC cap to $7. Consequently, the House bill would probably raise the significance of the role of the PFC relative to that of the AIP within the context of airport finance. S. 1451 does not raise the PFC cap.

Although neither H.R. 915 nor S. 1451 would restructure the AIP or PFC programs substantially, they would make a significant number of what may be seen as perfecting changes.

AIP Funding

The AIP authorization for FY2007, the final year of funding under Vision 100, was $3.7 billion. The authorization levels for FY2008 and FY2009 under the FAA extension bills were $3.675 billion and $3.9 billion, respectively.[1]

For FY2007, the amount actually made available through the appropriations process (i.e., the obligation limitation under P.L. 110-5) for AIP was $3.515 billion. In FY2008 and FY2009, the amount made available through the appropriations process was also $3.515 billion for each year (i.e., the obligation limitations under P.L. 110-161 and P.L. 111-8). Thus over time the difference between the authorized amounts and the amounts made available through the appropriations process has grown.

H.R. 915

The House bill (Section 101) would authorize AIP as follows: $4.0 billion for FY2010; $4.1 billion for FY2011; and $4.2 billion for FY2012. The $100 million annual growth in the program extends the pattern of funding growth in Vision 100. Over the three-year life of the bill, $12.3 billion would be authorized for AIP.

H.R. 915 would also rescind $305.5 million in unobligated amounts authorized for FY2009 and $102 million in unobligated amounts authorized for years previous to FY2009. However, because of the gap between the amounts authorized and the amounts made available for these fiscal years, it is doubtful that these rescissions will have a significant effect on the funding available for AIP.

S. 1451

S. 1451 (Section 104) would authorize AIP as follows: $4.0 billion for FY2010; $4.1 billion for FY2011. This matches the increases proposed in the House bill for these two years. Over the two-year life of the bill $8.1 billion would be authorized for AIP. S. 1451 includes no rescissions.

Formula Funding (Entitlements)

Primary Airport Entitlements

H.R. 915

The House bill does not include provisions altering the primary airport formulas. The bill does, however, include a provision (Section 140) related to the reduction of apportionments at large hub airports that charge PFCs above the $4.50 level. These airports would have their formula

---

[1] See P.L. 110-253 and P.L. 111-12.

apportionments (entitlements) reduced by 100% of the projected PFC revenues for the fiscal year, but not more than 100% of the amount than would otherwise be apportioned.

S. 1451

S. 1451 does not include provisions altering primary airport formulas.

Virtual Primary Airports

A special rule enacted after the September 11, 2001, terrorist attacks allowed some airports (referred to as virtual primary airports) whose annual passenger boardings fell below the required minimum passenger levels needed to maintain their primary airport status to continue receiving their annual primary airport entitlements (generally $1 million vs. the GA entitlement, which is generally $150,000). Earlier, the FY2006 Transportation/Treasury Appropriations Act (P.L. 109-115) extended the virtual primary airport eligibility through FY2006 but at a reduced entitlement of $500,000.

H.R. 915

The House bill includes no provisions regarding virtual primary airports.

S. 1451

Section 208(i) includes a special rule for airports whose enplanements fell, during 2008 or 2009, below the 10,000 threshold needed to qualify for primary airport entitlements, but had met the threshold during 2007. If these airports' enplanements for 2010 or 2011 decrease below 10,000 the Secretary of Transportation may make apportionments to these airports based on the amount the airports received for FY2009 (2008 and 2009 entitlements were based on 2007 enplanement data). During mark-up an additional provision was added for FY2008-2011 for airports with fewer than an average of 10,000 enplanements in 2004-2006.

As of this writing, CRS has been unable to determine the number of airports that would be eligible under S. 1451 for virtual primary entitlements. However, the difference for an airport between primary and GA entitlement funding is usually $850,000, so the provisions could have a significant impact on entitlement spending as well as the amount left over for discretionary grants once all the required entitlement distributions are satisfied.

General Aviation Entitlements

There are two components of the general aviation entitlements: the State Apportionment and the General Aviation apportionment (sometimes referred to as the Nonprimary Entitlement). Under current law 20% of AIP funds are to be apportioned for both components.

H.R. 915

The House bill (Section 139) would make changes in the general aviation entitlements. The state apportionment would be 10% of the amounts available for apportionment under AIP with a $300 million minimum. The nonprimary airport entitlement would remain $150,000 or one-fifth the estimated five-year development costs published in the most recent National Plan of Integrated Airport Systems (NPIAS). Should the 10% of amounts available for apportionment to the states fall below $300 million in a fiscal year (for this to happen the amounts available for apportionment for all of AIP would have to fall below $3 billion) the nonprimary entitlements would be reduced on a prorated basis to provide the funds to bring the state apportionment up to its $300 million minimum.

S. 1451

S. 1451 does not include a similar provision. GA entitlements would remain essentially the same as under current law.

State Block Grant Program

H.R. 915

The House bill (Section 502) would amend the state block grant program[2] by specifying that federal environmental requirements would apply to the program. The proposal specifies that any federal agency that grants any approval (i.e., permit or license) to a state must consult with that state during the approval process. Further, the federal agency would be required to use any state-prepared environmental analysis associated with that approval.

S. 1451

Section 209 of S. 1451 includes similar language to that in H.R. 915. It also includes a pilot program for up to three additional states that is consistent with the existing program.

Puerto Rico Minimum Guarantee

H.R. 915

The House bill (Section 151) provides a minimum entitlement for Puerto Rico, which guarantees that Puerto Rico shall receive at least 1.5% of the total amounts apportioned to all airports under 49 U.S.C. 47114 (c) and (d) for commercial service and general aviation airports.

S. 1451

S. 1451 includes no such provision.

---

[2] 49 U.S.C. § 47128.

United States Territory Minimum Guarantee

H.R. 915

The House bill includes no provision regarding a United States Territory Minimum Guarantee.

S. 1451

Section 217 would provide the Secretary of Transportation authority to raise the Territories' share of the total of primary and general aviation apportionments to 1.5%, if the total amounts flowing to the Territories through the normal apportionment process falls below that percentage.

Discretionary Funds

The discretionary fund includes the AIP funding that is not distributed under the apportioned entitlements as well as the forgone PFC revenues that are not directed to the small airport fund. Related PFC changes are discussed later in this report.

Minimum Discretionary Fund

49 U.S.C. 47115 requires that a minimum amount ($148 million plus any outstanding pre-January 1, 1997 letters of intent) remains available for the discretionary fund after all apportionments and set-asides are satisfied. If less money remains, the apportionments are reduced pro rata to provide funds to bring the discretionary funding up to the required level. Because AIP has been funded since FY2001 at historically high levels, the minimum discretionary fund provision has not recently been a factor in AIP funding.

H.R. 915

H.R. 915 (Section 141) sets the minimum amount to be credited to the discretionary fund at $520 million per year and drops the letter of intent language.

S. 1451

Section 208(k) includes the same provision as H.R. 915.

Noise Set-Aside

H.R. 915

The House bill (Section 143) would provide for a flat $300 million annual discretionary set-aside for AIP noise program costs in place of the current 35% discretionary set-aside.

S. 1451

Section 208 (h) includes the same provision as H.R. 915.

Military Airport Program (MAP)

H.R. 915

Retains the MAP as it exists under current law.

S. 1451

Section 212 adds consideration of whether or not a grant to the airport would be critical to the safety of commercial, military, or general aviation in trans-oceanic flights to MAP program selection considerations.

AIP Project Eligibility Changes

H.R. 915

The House bill makes a number of definitional and other changes that would impact AIP project eligibility. The bill includes provisions regarding eligibility of "revenue producing aeronautical support facilities" at nonprimary airports and the lowering of the passenger aircraft size required to meet the eligibility requirements for purchasing firefighting and rescue equipment. Terminal development is redefined to include development of an airport passenger terminal building, including gates and access roads and walkways servicing exclusively airport traffic that leads directly to or from the airport passenger terminal building. It also includes a provision regarding the construction of mobile refueler parking and clarifying definitions of general aviation airport and terminal development. The bill includes a provision regarding the relocation of airport-owned facilities. Under H.R. 915, repaying borrowed money for terminal development under 49 U.S.C. 47119(a) is clarified as an "airport development" and made eligible under certain circumstances. Projects to provide air conditioning, heating or electric power from terminal facilities to parked aircraft to reduce energy use and "harmful emissions," would be eligible. Airport planning would be redefined to include "developing an environmental management system." The cost of environmental review of airport-proposed environmentally beneficial aircraft flight procedures would also be AIP eligible.

S. 1451

Section 205 strikes 49 U.S.C. 47110 (d), "Terminal Development Costs," and replaces it with a subsection that makes the relocation of airport-owned facilities allowable for an airport development project, but only under certain conditions. Section 205 also appears to attempt to broaden the allowability of the use of non-primary entitlement funds for "facilities, as defined by Section 47102." Section 47102, however, does not appear to specifically define the term. Section 211 makes AIP eligible grants to an airport operator to assist in completing environmental review for environmentally-beneficial (mostly noise-related) aircraft flight procedures. Section 215 would make glycol (de-icing fluid) recovery vehicles eligible for AIP grants.

During mark-up of the bill by the Committee on Commerce, Science and Transportation an amendment was agreed upon to allow bird-detecting radar systems to be an eligible part of AIP project costs under certain conditions.

AIP Grant Assurances

H.R. 915

The House bill (Section 133) would make two changes to AIP grant assurances under 49 U.S.C. 47107. It allows for the use of AIP entitlement funds to replace or move a facility at an airport if the cause of the need was beyond the owner's control, such as a new design standard that made the present facility deemed a safety hazard.

The second proposed change deals with the disposition of profits made from the sale of land that was originally acquired for a noise compatibility purpose but is no longer needed for that purpose. Current law requires that the federal share of the proceeds, proportional to the federal share of the original land acquisition cost, be deposited in the trust fund. The proposed change would allow the proceeds to be reinvested in another project for, in preferential order: 1) an approved noise compatibility project at the airport; 2) an environmentally related project at the airport; 3) another eligible AIP project at the airport; 4) transfer to another airport for a noise compatibility project; or 5) payment to the trust fund.

S. 1451

Includes provisions similar to H.R. 915.

Federal Share

Under current law, the federal government share for AIP projects is as follows:

- 75% for large and medium hub airports (80% for noise compatibility projects);
- 95% for other airports;[3]
- "not more than" 95% for airport projects in states participating in the state block grant program; and
- 70% for projects funded from the discretionary fund at airports receiving exemptions under 49 U.S.C. Section 47134, the pilot program for private ownership of airports.

H.R. 915

H.R. 915 (Section 134) would provide a special rule to allow airports recently classified as medium hubs (which would drop their federal share to 75%) to retain their eligibility for an up to 90% federal share for a two year transition period.

H.R. 915 also includes a special rule for "Economically Depressed Communities." The rule would maintain the 95% federal share for projects at airports that are receiving subsidized service

---

[3] The temporary increase in share to 95% was established to provide relief to operators of small airports after the 9/11 terrorist attacks. The increase was to end on September 30, 2007, but has been continued under extension legislation. If the eventual multi-year reauthorization does not include a provision maintaining the 95% share, it will revert to 90%.

under the Essential Air Service (EAS) program that meet one or more of the criteria established in 42 U.S.C. 3161(a) as determined by the Secretary of Commerce. 42 U.S.C. 3161(a) sets forth three criteria for eligibility: 1) the area has a per capita income of 80 percent or less of the national average; 2) the area has an unemployment rate that is, for the most recent 24-month period for which data are available, at least 1% greater than the national average unemployment rate; and 3) the area is an area that the Secretary of Commerce determines has experienced or is about to experience a special need arising from actual or threatened severe unemployment or economic adjustment resulting from severe short-term or long-term changes in economic conditions. Given the variety of eligibility criteria and the rural location of EAS airports it is likely that many EAS airports could retain their 95% federal share under H.R. 915. Non-EAS airports (smaller than medium hub) would revert to 90% federal share under the bill.

S. 1451

Section 207 would provide for a 95% federal share for airports smaller than medium hub for the years FY2008, FY2009, FY2010, and FY2011. Block grant airports would also be provided with a 95% federal share. Section 204 would provide a special rule to allow airports recently classified as medium hubs (which would drop their federal share to 75%) to retain their eligibility for an up to 95% federal share for a two-year transition period.

Passenger Facility Charges (PFCs)

Increasing the PFC Cap

H.R. 915

Section 111 of the bill would allow for PFCs above the existing $4.50 cap at the $5, $6, and $7 levels. As is true under current law, only two PFCs could be charged during any single one-way trip, with a round-trip maximum of $28 (the current maximum is $18). As mentioned earlier, large hub airports imposing a PFC above the $4.50 level would forego from their AIP formula entitlements an amount equal to their projected PFC revenues but not more than 100% of the entitlement funding that otherwise would have been apportioned.

H.R. 915 includes a provision (Section 116) requiring a study of the impacts on airports of accommodating connecting passengers. The study is to include a recommendation as to whether different levels of PFCs should be imposed on connecting passengers versus origin and destination passengers. Some have argued that the PFC structure favors large hub airports' PFC revenues because the costs to an airport of a connecting passenger are less than those that primarily service originating Passengers.

S. 1451

Does not include an increase in the PFC cap.

Project Eligibility

H.R. 915

The bill (Section 112) includes a provision that would make eligible projects to construct secure bicycle storage facilities for use by passengers at the airport and that are in compliance with applicable security standards. One year after enactment FAA is to submit a report on progress made by airports to install bicycle parking.

In addition, H.R. 915 (Section 114) proposes a pilot program that would make available PFC funds for eligible intermodal ground access projects at five airports. The projects do not have to be on property owned or controlled by the sponsoring airport. The PFC project cost share would be limited to the projected ratio of airport-bound passengers to the total number of passengers using the ground access facility.

S. 1451

S. 1451 (Section 201) includes language that would make major changes to section 40117(d), which sets certain "limitations on approving applications." The bill would restrict the limitations to intermodal ground access projects, thereby freeing PFC applications for other types of projects from the limitations. The bill then also eliminates some of the current law limitations that would otherwise still apply to ground access projects. Among the limitations eliminated for all PFC applications is the requirement that the Secretary of DOT find that the project will meet at least one of the goals to: preserve or enhance capacity, safety, or security of the national air transportation system; reduce noise from an airport; or provide an opportunity for enhanced competition between or among air carriers and foreign air carriers. In addition, the bill would eliminate the precondition that for an airport to impose a fee above the $3 level the Secretary must find that the airport has made adequate provision for financing the airside needs of the airport, including runways, taxiways, aprons, and aircraft gates.

Competition Plans

Under current law no AIP or PFC grant may be approved for a large or medium hub airport unless the airport has submitted a written competition plan to the FAA.

H.R. 915

The House bill would extend the competition plan requirement.

S. 1451

The Senate bill is silent on the competition plan requirement.

Award of Architectural and Engineering Contracts for PFC Funded Airside Projects Made Subject to "Qualification-Based Selection" Procurement Requirements

H.R. 915

Section 113 of the bill appears to make any airside airport project supported by PFC-derived funds subject to Title IX of the Federal Property Administration Services Act of 1949, commonly known as the Brooks Act. Under the Brooks Act, consulting firms who provide engineering and architectural services are selected under "qualification-based selection" procedures. AIP professional service contracts already fall under the Brooks Act. Assuming the implementation of Section 113 would follow the AIP pattern, selections based on cost proposals would not be permitted if PFC funding is used to help pay the cost of consultant services. Fees for services would only be negotiated after the selection of the consulting firm is made.[4] Under AIP, a clear distinction is made between architectural and engineering contracts as opposed to contracts for aviation planning services.[5] Section 113, however, appears to combine planning and a variety of other administrative functions with architectural and engineering services. Unless clarified, this could lead to non-engineering services being reimbursed at the higher engineering overhead rate.[6]

S. 1451

The Senate bill does not include a similar provision.

Disadvantaged Business Enterprises Participation in PFC Funded Contracts

H.R. 915

Section 115 extends the application of requirements under 49 U.S.C. Parts 23 and 26 regarding the participation of disadvantaged business enterprises in contracts, subcontracts and business opportunities funded using PFCs and in airport concessions. It requires the Secretary of Transportation to issue regulations necessary to implement the provision.[7]

S. 1451

The Senate bill does not include a similar provision.

---

[4] See http://www.faa.gov/airports_airtraffic/airports/aip/procurement/professional_services/

[5] See Federal Aviation Administration, *Advisory Circular no. 150/5100-14D, Architectural, Engineering, and Planning Consultant Services for Airport Grant Projects*, http://www.airweb.faa.gov/Regulatory_and_Guidance_Library/rgAdvisoryCircular.nsf/0/87be820a72d12407862570a6006b4f29/$FILE/150-5100-14d.pdf

[6] One example of this is the case, under a contract funded with federal-aid highway funds, in which a consulting firm was reimbursed for the services of a typist at the engineer overhead rate. See http://www.projo.com/news/content/DOT_Employees_05-09-07_BN5IM6Q.35f046d.html

[7] For background on minority participation goals see, CRS Report RL33284, *Minority Contracting and Affirmative Action for Disadvantaged Small Businesses: Legal Issues*, by Jody Feder.

Passenger Facility Charge Pilot Program

H.R. 915

The House bill does not include this provision.

S. 1451

The Senate bill would establish a pilot program at up to six airports that would allow them to collect a PFC with no statutory ceiling on the fee. The fee, however, must be collected by the airport from the passenger. Under current law the PFCs are collected for the airports by the airlines during the ticketing process. GAO is to conduct a study of alternative means of collecting PFCs.

PFC Grant Streamlining and Revenue Diversion Provisions

H.R. 915

The House bill does not include a provision similar to the S. 1451.

S. 1451

Section 201 of the bill includes an extensive provision to streamline the PFC review and approval process. Instead of seeking approval on a project-by-project basis, for existing projects an airport would be required to submit to air carriers at the airport and to the FAA, and make available to the public, an annual PFC status report setting forth the airport's PFC revenues, spending, PFC funded projects, the next year's projected revenues, and a description of the consultation and public notice process. Once the status report is submitted no further action is required and implementation could continue. For new projects, the airport would have to provide for a notice and comment period for carriers operating at the airport and a public notice and comment period before they file their PFC status report. Once the report is filed the airport could begin collecting the new PFC. Stakeholders could, however, file objections, and if the FAA agrees with the objection, the FAA could terminate the airport's authority to collect PFC revenues for the project. The proposal also provides that DOT may investigate whether a PFC charge is excessive or whether PFC revenue is being diverted to non-allowable uses.

In the case of an airport found to have diverted revenue, the airport may not propose collection or use of a PFC unless DOT determines that the airport has taken corrective action to address the violation.

Other Airport-Related Provisions

Privatization

The Airport Privatization Pilot Program allows FAA to exempt five airports from federal requirements relating to the use of airport revenue. The requirement that airport revenue be expended for aviation purposes is seen as a major inhibitor of airport privatization. Since the program was enacted in 1996 (Section 149 of the Federal Aviation Reauthorization Act of 1996, P.L. 104-264), only one airport has been privatized, Stewart International Airport (New York), although the privatization of Chicago Midway is pending. Supporters of privatization have argued that the current pilot program gives airlines effective veto power over privatization transactions. Current law requires that the airport sponsor may only recover from the sale or lease the amount that may be approved by at least 65% of the air carriers serving the airport; and by air carriers that account for 65% of the total landed weight at the airport for the year.

H.R. 915

The bill (Section 145) would raise the required air carrier approval percentages from 65% to 75%. Airports participating in the pilot program would not be eligible for AIP funds.

S. 1451

The Senate bill does not include this provision.

Airport Development Rights Pilot Program—Sunset Provision

This pilot program allows for the purchase of a privately owned public use airport's development rights as a means of keeping the airport open and operating. FAA argues that the program has not been a success and suggests a better strategy would be to find a public sponsor to purchase the airport rather than just the development rights. Some general aviation supporters may still be supportive of the pilot program.

H.R. 915

The bill (Section 147) includes a sunset provision that sets the end of the Airport Development Rights Pilot program as September 30, 2008.

S. 1451

The Senate bill does not include similar language.

Pilot Program for Redevelopment of Airport Properties

H.R. 915

The House bill (Section 817) requires that within a year of enactment the FAA is to establish a trial program at up to four public-use airports that have approved noise compatibility programs under 49 U.S.C. 47102. Under this trial program, the FAA may make grants from the discretionary noise set-aside funds under 49 U.S.C. 47117(e)(1)(A) to support joint planning, engineering, and environmental permitting to facilitate the assembly and redevelopment of real property purchased with noise mitigation funds made available under the AIP or PFC programs. The trial program is to encourage compatible land uses with the airport and generate economic benefits to both the airport operator and the affected local jurisdiction.

S. 1451

Section 712 of the Senate bill includes a similar provision, although the grant requirement and limitations vary somewhat.

Solid Waste Recycling Plans

H.R. 915

Section 132 requires that for any airport with a master plan to receive AIP funding, the plan must address the feasibility of solid waste recycling and minimizing the generation of solid waste at the airport.

S. 1451

Section 714 includes language similar to that in H.R. 915.

Airport Disadvantaged Business Enterprise Program

H.R. 915

Section 137 requires the Secretary of Transportation to establish a program to eliminate barriers to small business participation in airport-related contracts and concessions by prohibiting excessive, unreasonable, or discriminatory bonding requirement for any project funded under AIP or using passenger facility charge revenues under section 40117.

The Secretary of Transportation must issue a final rule establishing the program one year after the date of enactment.

Also, not later than 180 days after the date of enactment, the Secretary shall issue final regulations to adjust the personal net worth cap used in determining whether an individual is economically disadvantaged, to correct for the impact of inflation since the cap was set at $750,000 in 1989. Thereafter, annually on June 30, the Secretary shall adjust the cap to account for changes in the Consumer Price Index of All Urban Consumers for the previous 12 months.

S. 1451

S. 1451 includes provisions similar to H.R. 915.

Training Program for Certification of Disadvantaged Business Enterprises

H.R. 915

Section 138 requires that the Secretary of Transportation establish a training program for officials or agents of airport sponsors that are responsible for certifying that the airport owner or operator will meet its minority set-aside goal or who are responsible for determining whether or not a small business qualifies as being owned and controlled by socially or economically disadvantaged individuals. $2 million is authorized annually to carry out the provision. Not later than 24 months after the date of enactment the Secretary shall submit a report to the House Transportation and Infrastructure Committee and the Senate Committee on Commerce, Science, and Transportation on the results of the training program.

S. 1451

Section 715 of the Senate bill includes a similar provision.

Metropolitan Washington Airports Authority

H.R. 915

The House bill has no provision concerning the Metropolitan Washington Airports Authority.

S. 1451

An amendment, agreed to in full committee mark-up, this provision would repeal 49 U.S.C. 49108, which prevents the Metropolitan Washington Airports Authority from applying for AIP or PFC grants after October 1, 2008.

Spending Guarantee Mechanisms

Since the 1971 creation of the user-supported airport and airway trust fund there has been disagreement over the appropriate use of the trust fund's revenues. This led, beginning in 1976, to the enactment of a series of legislative mechanisms designed to assure that federal capital spending for U.S. airports and airways (i.e., AIP and F&E) would be funded at their fully authorized levels. For a detailed discussion of the history and impact of the various spending guarantee mechanisms, see CRS Report RL33654, *Aviation Spending Guarantee Mechanisms*, by Robert S. Kirk.

The current mechanism dates back to 2000 and includes two spending guarantees. One makes it out-of-order in the House or Senate to consider legislation that fails to use all aviation trust fund receipts and interest annually. The second makes it out-of-order to consider any bill that provided any funding for RE&D or O&M if the bill fails to fully fund AIP and F&E at their authorized levels. The current guarantees will lapse at the end of FY2009 if no further action is taken to extend them.

H.R. 915

The House bill (Section 105) would amend the airport and airway trust fund guarantee that requires that the total amounts made available from the trust fund be equal to the level of receipts plus interest for the year. Under H.R. 915, for FY2010, the amounts made available would equal 90% of the estimated level of receipts plus interest on the fund for the fiscal year. For FY2011 and FY2012, the guaranteed level would equal the sum of 90% of the estimated receipts plus interest for each respective year, plus the difference between the actual receipts and total amounts made available for obligation from two years before (i.e., FY2009 and FY2010, respectively). The bill would retain the point-of-order enforcement mechanisms.

This change would have a number of possible implications. First, the change could lessen the demands on trust fund revenues for the first two years of the reauthorization, allowing a modest accumulation in the unexpended balance of the trust fund during these years. Second, it would reduce the likelihood that overly optimistic revenue projections could lead to spending at rates that exceed the actual revenues accruing to the trust fund (as has happened in recent years), at least in the first year of the bill. Finally, by limiting trust fund spending, the change could, in the minds of some, increase the likelihood that the general fund contribution percentage for the FAA budget could be set at a higher level.

S. 1451

The Senate bill is silent on the spending guarantee.

FAA Management and Organizational Issues

Management and organizational reform at the FAA has been a central focus of both legislative and administration initiatives over the past several years. Central issues include

- Measures designed to achieve better integration of NGATS/NextGen planning and implementation into the FAA's ongoing planning and acquisition activities;

- Measures to establish a mechanism for considering possible realignment and consolidation of various FAA facilities and services; and

- Provisions to increase the flexibility in the design and implementation of NGATS/NextGen by allowing airports and private entities to play a more direct role in acquiring, deploying, and maintaining facilities and services to augment the FAA's air traffic communications, navigation, and surveillance capabilities.

These issues, and the related legislative proposals under consideration in the current FAA reauthorization debate, are discussed in further detail below.

Planning and Oversight of Next Generation Air Transportation System Development

A central issue permeating the current reauthorization debate is the adequacy of management and organizational processes to facilitate development of NextGen. NextGen is being developed to address system-wide capacity needs, and is scheduled to be completed prior to 2025. A provision in Vision 100 created the multi-agency Joint Planning and Development Office (JPDO) and charged it with the task of defining, developing, and implementing the Next Generation Air Transportation System (NGATS) or NextGen plan.

Over the past three years, the JPDO has collaborated with governmental and industry partners to draft a concept for NextGen development. Some critics have argued that the pace of this effort has been too slow, while others have voiced concern that the scope of the JPDO concept—encompassing "curbside-to-curbside" movement of airline passengers, rather than just block-to-block handling of all aircraft types within the national airspace system—may be inappropriate. Still others have raised concerns over the organizational and management structure of the JPDO, specifically regarding the JPDO's potential lack of influence over management and budgetary processes of participating agencies. While these agencies are ultimately charged with the task of carrying out the engineering work to build NextGen as well as the operational responsibilities to run and maintain the national airspace system and its many components, including, but not limited to air traffic control services and airport security functions, the link between their respective budgets and the NextGen program is not clearly defined.

Various options to address these concerns that have been identified include establishing a lead systems integration (LSI) entity to oversee the engineering of NextGen systems, or possibly establishing specific reporting requirements, perhaps through the budget and appropriations process, in which the various agencies involved could identify how budgetary elements would support NextGen development and how cross-agency efforts would be coordinated and aligned.

H.R. 915

H.R. 915 includes sense of Congress language recognizing that modernizing the air transportation system is a national priority. To address this need to prioritize investment in the Next Generation Air Transportation System (NGATS), the bill includes several provisions designed to improve the management and implementation of this effort.

H.R. 915 would establish the JPDO director as a voting member of the FAA's Joint Resources Council. The bill would give the JPDO director the title Associate Administrator for the Next Generation Air Transportation System, a position that would report directly to the FAA Administrator. To the extent possible, the JPDO director would be required to oversee development of the integrated NGATS plan, ensuring that each federal agency involved has requested sufficient funds in the annual budget process to carry out its responsibilities under the plan. The JPDO director would also be responsible for making sure that the development and implementation of NGATS stays on schedule, and identify and justify in the President's budget submission any inconsistencies between the NGATS plan and the budget request.

H.R. 915 would also require each component agency involved in the NGATS initiative to designate a senior official responsible for carrying out NGATS-related activities of the agency, serving as a liaison for the agency in matters involving NGATS support, and ensuring that the agency meets its obligations set forth in memoranda of understanding regarding NGATS development and support. The bill further requires that the JPDO work with the OMB to develop a process for identifying projects tied to the NGATS program across all affiliated federal agencies and consider the NGATS as a cross-agency, unified program.

Further, H.R. 915 would require a multiagency integrated work plan for NGATS including an outline of activities required to achieve the end-state architecture defined in the program's concept of operations (CONOPS); year-by-year details of accomplishments, activities, research, requirements, rulemakings, policy decisions, and other milestones; an outline of annual objectives and responsible agencies; an estimate of year-by-year funding requirements for each development stage; and "a clear explanation of how each step in the development of [NGATS] will lead to the following step and the implications of not successfully completing a step in the time period described in the integrated work plan." The bill would also require the FAA to issue a "NextGen Implementation Plan," detailing how the agency is implementing NGATS, on an annual basis as well as annual reports to the congressional oversight committees detailing progress made in carrying out the multiagency integrated NGATS work plan. Also, under H.R. 915, the NGATS Senior Policy Committee would be required to meet twice each year and prepare an annual report to coincide with the President's budget request detailing progress made on the multiagency integrated NGATS work plan and any changes to that plan, detailing the impact of those changes.

H.R. 915 would also require GAO to review the progress and challenges of transforming the national airspace system to NGATS, and review ongoing air traffic modernization projects and progress on NGATS component systems including En Route Automation Modernization (ERAM); Standard Terminal Automation Replacement System/Common Automated Radar Terminal Systems (STARS/CARTS); Traffic Flow Management Modernization (TFM-M); System Wide Information Management (SWIM); and ADS-B. The bill would also task the National Research Council with performing a review of the enterprise architecture for the NGATS examining technical activities, program risk, and opportunities to mitigate risk based on experiences with other complex, software-intensive systems. The bill would also require the FAA, in consultation with other agencies such as NASA, to initiate a research program on methods to improve and streamline the process of certifying new technologies for introduction into the national airspace system. The bill also authorizes additional appropriations, totaling $56.8 million over the four-year authorization period, specifically for airspace redesign initiatives to enhance aviation system capacity and reduce delays.

S. 1451

Title III of S. 1451 includes numerous provisions related to the management and oversight of FAA air traffic modernization initiatives and NextGen technology deployment. The FAA would be required to issue a NextGen implementation plan within six months of enactment that would be updated annually and must include a schedule of rulemaking pertaining to regulations and guidelines for implementing NextGen.

The bill seeks to create an Air Traffic Control Modernization Oversight Board made up of the Administrator, a Department of Defense (DoD) representative, someone representing the public interest, and individuals representing various aviation interests including airports; passenger or cargo air carriers; aircraft manufacturers; FAA labor organizations; and general aviation. Board members would be appointed by the President with the advice and consent of the Senate to serve four-year terms. The board would be responsible for reviewing and advising the FAA regarding modernization programs, the annual NextGen Implementation Plan and budget, cost accounting practices, the strategic plan for modernization, and the operational efficiency of the air traffic control system. The board would be required to approve air traffic equipment purchases over $100 million, the FAA's annual budget request for facilities and equipment, the FAA's annual Capital Investment Plan (CIP).

S. 1451 also seeks to create a new NextGen management structure led by a Chief NextGen Officer, selected by the FAA Administrator with the approval of the proposed Air Traffic Control Modernization Oversight Board. The Chief NextGen Officer would be responsible for overseeing the implementation of all FAA NextGen programs, developing an annual NextGen implementation plan, and overseeing JPDO's facilitation of cooperation among participating federal agencies. The Senate bill seeks to modify the managerial structure and responsibilities of the JPDO, referring to it instead as the NextGen System Implementation Office, which would be headed by a director that would report to the Chief NextGen Officer. Other agencies engaged in NextGen development would be required to designate an agency NextGen implementation officer to oversee the respective agencies activities related to NextGen development, liaison and coordinate with other agencies on NextGen implementation, and manage agency projects, staffing and budgets tied to NextGen. Within six months of enactment, each of the agencies would be required to issue memoranda of understanding with other participating agencies describing the responsibilities, budgetary commitments, and staffing resources of each agency devoted to NextGen implementation.

S. 1451 also includes language designed to accelerate NextGen technology deployment. Specifically, the bill would require the FAA to issue a report within six months of enactment detailing its strategy for developing, certifying, and implementing Required Navigational Performance (RNP) and area navigation (RNAV) capabilities/procedures, which exploit satellite navigation technologies, to maximize efficiency and capacity at the nation's busiest airports. The bill sets a implementation schedule that would require completion of 30% of the procedures within 18 months of enactment, 60% within 36 months, and 100% by January 1, 2014. The bill would also require the FAA to issue a report by January 1, 2014, detailing its plan for expanding RNAV/RNP capabilities to other airports, and sets a timeframe that would require 25% of planned procedures to be implemented by 2015, 50% by 2016, 75% by 2017, and 100% by 2018. A separate provision of the bill would require the FAA to set a target of commissioning 200 RNP procedures annually through FY2012, with 25% of these meeting low visibility approach criteria objectives established in the NextGen Implementation Plan. In establishing priorities for these implementation schedules, the bill directs the FAA to expand the charter of the Performance Based Navigation Aviation Rulemaking Committee as needed to establish priorities based on their potential benefits with regard to improving safety and alleviating airport and airspace congestion. The bill also would require the FAA to submit its plan for a nationwide communications systems to congressional oversight committees within one year of enactment. The bill also calls for a report evaluating the impact of NextGen technologies on more efficient use of airspace, reduced fuel consumption, and reduced aircraft emissions. The FAA would also be required to assess the feasibility of reducing aircraft separation standards without compromising safety, and if deemed feasible, develop a timetable for implementation of reduced separation standards.

The bill would also require the FAA to submit a report to the congressional oversight committees detailing its program and schedule for integrating ADS-B into the National Airspace System, including a clearly defined budget, schedule, and a transition plan with clearly defined milestones. In the report, the FAA would be required to identify any potential workforce and operational changes expected to result from ADS-B deployment as well as a timeline for implementing advanced operational procedures exploiting ADS-B capabilities, including ADS-B air-to-air features. The report would be required to assess the benefits derived from ADS-B deployment. The Senate bill would require the FAA to finalize its rulemaking proceeding regarding requirements for ADS-B equipage of aircraft, and would accelerate requirements for aircraft operators to install ADS-B Out (i.e., transmission only) capabilities by 2015, pending verification by the Air Traffic Control Modernization Oversight Board that the necessary ADS-B ground infrastructure is in place and properly functioning, that certification standards for aircraft ADS-B equipment have been approved, and that such equipment interfaces safely and efficiently with ADS-B infrastructure. The bill also would require the equipage of aircraft with ADS-B In (i.e., receive capability) by 2018. Toward reaching this objective of full-scale ADS-B deployment by 2018, the bill would require operational testing of ADS-B in congested airspace, identification of required equipment and training for air traffic controllers, and the development of procedures for air traffic management in environments where there is a mix of ADS-B and radar-based air traffic monitoring. The bill would also require the FAA to issue a report identifying incentive options that would encourage operators to equip aircraft with NextGen technologies, including development of policies that would give priority to ADS-B equipped aircraft.

S. 1451 would also require the FAA to adopt and monitor a series of performance metrics to gauge the efficiency of the National Airspace System. The bill specifies that, at a minimum, these metrics are to include allowable operations per hour on runways; average gate-to-gate times; fuel burned between city pairs; numbers and percentages of operations using advanced RNAV/RNP and ADS-B procedures; average distance flown between key city pairs; times between pushback and takeoff; flights that proceed using an uninterrupted or continuous climb or descent; average gate arrival delay for all arrivals; actual versus planned flight times for key city pairs; and metrics to demonstrate reduced fuel burn and reduced aircraft emissions. The FAA would be required to establish baseline levels for each of these metrics, make all data publicly available, and issue annual progress reports.

Within six months of enactment, S. 1451 would require the FAA to develop a plan for streamlining and accelerating the process for certifying NextGen technologies, addressing factors such as manufacturing, installation, operational procedures, pilot and controller training, and staffing needs. The FAA would be required to assess the extent to which third parties will be used in the certification process, and the cost and benefits of relying on third parties.

Realignment and Consolidation of FAA Facilities and Operations

The FAA's reauthorization proposal introduced in the 110th Congress (see H.R. 1356/S. 1076, 110th Congress) outlined a process for evaluating and implementing recommended FAA facility and service consolidation in a manner designed to minimize political influence on the process, much like the military BRAC process, which it is closely modeled after. The overall objective would be to identify and implement recommended realignment and consolidation activities that would help reduce FAA capital, operating, maintenance, and administrative costs without adversely impacting system safety.

The FAA proposal includes details of the process and a timeline for carrying out a system-wide review and implementation of realignment and consolidation of FAA facilities and services. While the proposed process closely follows the military BRAC process, which has generally been regarded as a successful approach to realignment and consolidation of military bases and units, the prospect of implementing such a process to assess FAA facilities and services may be regarded as controversial during the reauthorization debate, particularly in local regions that may stand to lose FAA facilities and jobs as an outcome of the process. Consideration of the process in legislation may also be opposed by labor organizations representing FAA employees, although nothing in current statute generally prohibits the FAA from engaging in organizational consolidation and realignment.

H.R. 915

In contrast to the FAA proposal offered by the Bush Administration, H.R. 915 proposes to establish an FAA working group, similar to an advisory group, to develop criteria and make recommendations for realignment of services and facilities. Members of the nine-member working group would consist of the FAA Administrator, two airline representatives, two airport representatives, two representatives from the general aviation community, and two labor organization representatives representing FAA regional office or field employees. An amendment agreed to and incorporated into the House-passed version of the bill would require that FAA regional office consolidation be included in the scope of the working group's oversight. That provision also stipulates that the working group members from labor unions representing FAA employees may be selected from unions representing employees working at either field facilities or regional offices.

The FAA would be required to form the working group within nine months of enactment, and once established, the working group would have six months to develop criteria and recommendations for realignment and present those findings to the appropriate congressional oversight committees. The working group's report is to include justifications for each recommendation to consolidate or realign specific facilities and services, including associated costs and savings estimates. In addition to providing the report to the congressional committees, the report would be published in the Federal Register allowing 45 days for public comments and written objections to the recommendations contained in the report.

Sixty days after the close of the public comment period, the FAA Administrator would be required to submit a second report to the congressional oversight committees detailing the Administrator's recommendations for consolidation and realignment, along with copies of any public comments and objections received. The statute would bar the Administrator from implementing any consolidation or realignment of facilities or services until this report is submitted. However, once the report is submitted, this does not otherwise limit the Administrator's authority to initiate proposed actions or require that these actions be subject to any further review.

H.R. 915 also calls for the creation of an 12-member task force on air traffic control facility conditions. Eight members of the task force would be selected by the FAA administration, and four would be chosen by labor unions representing employees that work at these field facilities. Four members would be required to be experts on various hazardous building conditions, while two members would be required to have expertise in rehabilitating aging buildings. Members would be appointed for the duration of the task force's existence. They would not be compensated for their membership, but would be reimbursed for travel expenses related to the work of the task force. Under the provision, the task force would be permitted to hire personnel as needed, and state and federal employees may be detailed to work on the task force. The task force would be responsible for studying the conditions of all air traffic control facilities, facility condition indices (FCIs), reports of respiratory ailments of other conditions within these facilities, facility conditions that could interfere with job performance, and available scientifically approved remediation techniques and their application. Based on its study, the task force would be required to issue recommendations to prioritize facility rehabilitation, ensure that the FAA utilizes scientifically approved remediation techniques, and assist the FAA in making programmatic changes to prevent facilities from deteriorating to unsafe levels.

S. 1451

S. 1451 would require the FAA to allow for public comment on and publish within nine months of enactment details of the final criteria to be used in making its recommendations regarding the realignment of services and facilities intended to assist in the transition to NextGen facilities and to reduce costs without compromising safety. Within nine months of enactment, the FAA would also be required to publish a formal list of services and facilities recommended for realignment, including a justification and cost savings analysis for each. If requested, the FAA would be required to hold a public hearing regarding the proposed realignment in any community that would be affected by its recommendations. Upon release of these recommendations, the proposed Air Traffic Control Modernization Oversight Board, discussed above, would be required to review and analyze the FAA's recommendations along with public comments regarding these recommendations. Based on this review and analysis, the Board would make its own independent recommendations for realignment of aviation facilities and services that would be submitted in a report to the President and to congressional oversight committees. The legislation would explicitly prohibit consolidation of facilities into the Southern California Terminal Radar Approach Control (TRACON) facility, the Northern California TRACON, the Memphis TRACON, and the Miami TRACON until the Board's recommendations are completed. S. 1451 also contains a provision that would require the FAA to establish a process for including employees selected from collective bargaining units likely to be affected by air traffic modernization projects, including NextGen initiatives, in the planning, development, and implementation of such projects.

S. 1451 would also require the FAA to convene a task force on air traffic control facility conditions. The task force, to be comprised of seven members appointed by the Administrator and four members appointed by labor unions representing field facility employees, would be required to have four specialists on toxic mold abatement, "sick building syndrome," and other building health hazards, and two specialists with expertise on rehabilitating aging buildings. The task force would be required to study the conditions of all air traffic control facilities in the United States; review reports of employees working in these facilities related to respiratory ailments and other facility-related health conditions; assess conditions of the facilities that may interfere with job performance and safety; the ability of managers and supervisors to document and seek remediation for unsafe facility conditions; whether employees reporting facility related illnesses are treated fairly; whether scientifically approved remediation techniques are implemented in a timely fashion when hazardous facility conditions are identified; and FAA resources for facility maintenance and renovation. Based on its study, the task force shall make recommendations, within six months of its formation, regarding the prioritization of facilities with respect to remediation and renovation to address employee health and safety, methods for ensuring that scientifically approved remediation techniques are used to correct problems at all affected facilities; and programmatic changes to prevent aging air traffic control facilities from deteriorating to unsafe levels. Within 30 days of receiving the task force study and recommendations, the FAA would be required to report to the congressional oversight committees regarding its plan, timeline, and budgetary requirements and priorities for addressing the task force's recommendations.

Air Traffic Controller and Technical Staffing and Training

Amid growing numbers of retiring controllers and the pending shift toward integrating NextGen technologies in the air traffic control environment, there is growing policy interest in the staffing of air traffic facilities and the training of air traffic controllers and systems specialists that maintain air traffic control technologies. Besides the need to train controllers to operate new NextGen systems, the mix of fully certified controllers and developmental controllers (i.e., controllers still completing on-the-job training to obtain full certification) has become a growing issue, particularly as the FAA faces a near-term transition in the controller workforce with large numbers of retirements anticipated over the next three to five years.

H.R. 915

H.R. 915 would require the National Academy of Sciences to carry out a study examining human factors, traffic activity, and air traffic control technology and based on this study make recommendations for the development of FAA staffing standards for air traffic controllers. The bill also would require the FAA to study the adequacy of training programs for air traffic controllers examining current training and required competencies as well as available training approaches and required competencies for NextGen operations. H.R. 915 would also require a study looking at alternative training approaches for new controllers hired through the Collegiate Training Initiative (CTI), which provides undergraduate training designed to prepare students for a career as an air traffic controller.

S. 1451

S. 1451 directs the FAA to carry out a comprehensive review and evaluation of the FAA Academy, where newly hired controllers undergo initial training. The provision also directs the FAA to examine facility training of developmental controllers, who have graduated from the academy but are not yet fully qualified and certified to control air traffic on their own. The measure would require the FAA to establish standards for the number of developmental controllers that can be accommodated at each FAA facility based on the available number of on-the-job instructors, the number and availability of classrooms and simulators, training requirements, and current levels of controllers already in training. The bill would also require a GAO study of the FAA's program of training for airway transportation systems specialists that maintain ATC technology infrastructure. The report would examine current training curricula, training needs for maintaining proficiency in the latest technology, distribution and cost of in-house and vendor training, and recommendations for cost effective approaches for providing up-to-date training on the latest technologies. A provision of the bill would also require the FAA to carry out a study of front-line manager staffing at air traffic facilities, taking into account factors such as facility type, traffic complexity, controller proficiency, and training requirements.

Partnerships for Next Generation Technology Deployment

An option under consideration is to allow private sector investment in communications, navigation, surveillance and other services provided within the context of the national airspace system. For example, under such provisions, telecommunications providers may opt to deploy technologies to augment in-cockpit air traffic surveillance capabilities and datalink weather and other flight-related information to airborne aircraft. Under such a scheme, these providers may be able to offer certain fee-for-service capabilities to aircraft to augment a core set of required aircraft communication, navigation, and surveillance capabilities. Another option being considered is to allow for airport ownership and control of certain communications, navigation, and surveillance equipment that has been historically acquired, deployed, and maintained by the FAA.

H.R. 915

H.R. 915 authorizes the creation of a public-private partnership that includes a "university component with significant aviation expertise in air traffic management, simulation, meteorology, and engineering and aviation business" to serve as an airport-based testing site for existing NGATS technologies. The provision stipulates that the testing site should serve a mix of both commercial and general aviation traffic. Also, H.R. 915 would establish a NextGen Research and Development Center of Excellence. The center would be responsible for leveraging the FAA's centers of excellence program, a program that relies on several university consortia to address ongoing FAA research and development challenges, to enhance the development of NGATS technologies within academia and industry. The NextGen Research and Development Center of

Excellence would be responsible for providing educational, technical, and analytical assistance to the FAA and other agencies involved in NGATS development, such as NASA and the DoD, to aid in the research and development of NGATS technologies.

H.R. 915 also includes language that would require the FAA to establish a process for including certain FAA employees, selected by their respective collective bargaining units, along with other stakeholders that are likely to be impacted by the NGATS development and other modernization initiatives in the planning, development, and deployment of ATC modernization projects. This may include air traffic controllers and airway system specialists that maintain ATC infrastructure, who have expressed concern that they have not been adequately included in the planning and conceptualization of NGATS and in the development of other modernization initiatives. These employees would serve in a collaborative, advisory capacity and, in addition to regular compensation and benefits, would receive travel and per diem expenses in accordance with FAA travel policies while serving in this capacity.

H.R. 915 would also require the FAA to prepare a report on the program and schedule for integrating ADS-B into the national airspace system. The report is to include detailed information on protections and contingencies that would be included in any FAA contracts to cover the event of a contractor's default, bankruptcy, acquisition, or other event that may jeopardize the uninterrupted delivery of ADS-B services. The provision further specifies that any FAA contract for ADS-B services contain contingencies requiring: FAA Administrator approval of any assignment of the contract or assumption of the contract vendor by another entity; designation of ADS-B assets as critical national infrastructure for security purposes; continuation of ADS-B broadcast services for a reasonable period following a contract termination or in the event of material nonperformance, until another vendor can begin providing these services; and permission for the federal government to acquire or utilize the ADS-B contractor assets to ensure uninterrupted ADS-B services, provided that reasonable compensation for use of such assets is made.

H.R. 915 would require the Department of Transportation's Office of Inspector General (DOT OIG) to conduct a review of the effectiveness of FAA oversight in connection with third party development of flight procedures, such as instrument approaches to airports. The review would include an assessment of the degree to which the FAA is relying on plans to utilize third parties for developing flight procedures, and whether there is adequate FAA staff and processes to assess the safety of these third-party activities. The report is to also assess whether the FAA has sufficient internal staffing and resources to meet the needs for safely and efficiently developing flight procedures without the use of third-party resources.

S. 1451

S. 1451 includes language that would require the FAA to assess the costs and benefits of using third parties to assist in the development of RNP and RNAV procedures for increasing capacity and efficiency of the national airspace system. The FAA would also be required to assess the costs and benefits of using third parties to develop and verify certification standards for NextGen technologies. A separate provision of the bill would specifically authorize the FAA to give third parties the ability to design, flight check, and implement RNP procedures. Similar to H.R. 915, the bill instructs the DOT OIG to carry out assessments of third-party agreements for developing new operational and approach procedures, focusing on whether the FAA has established sufficient mechanisms and allocated sufficient staffing to provide safety oversight of these activities.

S. 1451 would also establish cooperative agreements with up to five states under a test program for creating ADS-B equipage banks that would provide loans and other assistance to public entities for equipping aircraft with ADS-B and other related NextGen avionics. Each bank would be required to fund each account with 50% of a project's funds derived from nonfederal sources. Each bank would be required to maintain an investment grade rating on its debt issuances or maintain sufficient bonds or insurance to maintain viability. Investment income, derived from investing in U.S. Treasury securities, bank deposits, or other DOT-approved financial instruments, would be credited to the ADS-B equipage account and made available for providing loans and assistance for eligible ADS-B equipage projects at below market interest rates. Loan repayment terms under this proposed program would not be allowed to exceed 10 years. The bill would authorize $25 million per year for FY2010 through FY2014 for providing the federal funding to these ADS-B equipage banks.

FAA Personnel Management

In 1995, Congress authorized the Administrator of the FAA to develop a new personnel management system for the agency's workforce. Section 347(a) of the Department of Transportation and Related Agencies Appropriations Act, 1996, provided for the development and implementation of this personnel management system following consultation with FAA employees and any non-governmental experts in personnel management systems employed by the Administrator.[8] The system was intended to provide for "greater flexibility in the hiring, training, compensation, and location of personnel."[9] As enacted originally, chapter 71 of Title 5 of the U.S. Code, relating to labor-management relations in most federal agencies, did not apply to the new personnel management system.[10] However, in March 1996, Congress amended section 347 to make chapter 71 applicable to this system.[11]

In October 1996, Congress considered additional requirements for the FAA personnel management system. Section 253 of the Federal Aviation Reauthorization Act of 1996 amended title 49 of the U.S. Code to add a new section involving consultation and negotiation with respect to the new system.[12] 49 U.S.C. § 40122(a) provides, in relevant part:

> (1) Consultation and Negotiation—In developing and making changes to the personnel management system initially implemented by the Administrator of the Federal Aviation Administration on April 1, 1996, the Administrator shall negotiate with the exclusive bargaining representatives of employees of the Administration certified under section 7111 of title 5 and consult with other employees of the Administration.

> (2) Mediation—If the Administrator does not reach an agreement under paragraph (1) with the exclusive bargaining representatives, the services of the Federal Mediation and Conciliation Service shall be used to attempt to reach such agreement. If the services of the Federal Mediation and Conciliation Service do not lead to an agreement, the Administrator's proposed change to the personnel management system shall not take effect until 60 days

---

[8] P.L. 104-50, § 347(a), 109 Stat. 436, 460 (1995).

[9] *Id.*

[10] *See* P.L. 104-50, § 347(b), 109 Stat. 436, 460 (1995) (identifying provisions of title 5, U.S. Code, that would be applicable to the new personnel management system).

[11] P.L. 104-122, § 1, 110 Stat. 876 (1996).

[12] P.L. 104-264, § 253, 110 Stat. 3213, 3237 (1996).

have elapsed after the Administrator has transmitted the proposed change, along with the objections of the exclusive bargaining representatives to the change, and the reasons for such objections, to Congress.

In the report that accompanied the Senate version of the 1996 Act, the Senate Committee on Commerce, Science, and Transportation indicated that "[i]n negotiating changes to the personnel system, the Administrator and the exclusive bargaining representatives would be required to use every reasonable effort to find cost savings and to increase productivity within each of the affected bargaining units, as well as within the FAA as a whole."[13] The House version of the act did not include a provision on consultation, negotiation, and mediation. The Senate provisions were incorporated into the final version of the legislation during conference.[14]

In 2005, a federal district court considered the impact of 49 U.S.C. § 40122 on labor-management relations at the FAA.[15] After reaching bargaining impasses with the FAA, the National Air Traffic Controllers Association ("NATCA") and the Professional Airways Systems Specialists ("PASS") sought the assistance of the Federal Service Impasses Panel ("FSIP"), an entity within the Federal Labor Relations Authority ("FLRA") that provides assistance with resolving negotiation impasses between federal agencies and unions. In 2004, unclear about whether it had the authority to resolve impasses involving the FAA in light of 49 U.S.C. § 40122, FSIP declined to provide assistance.[16]

After reviewing the development of the FAA personnel management system and the enactment of 49 U.S.C. § 40122, the district court concluded that complaints related to an agency's participation in FSIP's impasse resolution procedures could be deemed an unfair labor practice.[17] Consequently, the court declared that "[w]hen agency action constitutes an arguable unfair labor practice, jurisdiction rests exclusively with the Authority and the Courts of Appeals.... For these reasons, the [court] concludes that it is without jurisdiction and should defer to the FLRA."[18]

Although the FLRA did not address the matter, the U.S. Court of Appeals for the District of Columbia Circuit did review the district court opinion in February 2006. In *National Air Traffic Controllers Association v. Federal Services Impasses Panel*, the D.C. Circuit affirmed the district court decision, concluding that FSIP did not have a clear and specific statutory mandate to assert jurisdiction over the parties' bargaining impasses.[19] The court did observe, however, that the FAA's refusal to participate in proceedings before FSIP could form the basis of an unfair labor practice charge before the FLRA.[20]

On April 5, 2006, the FAA announced formally that it had reached an impasse in its negotiations with NATCA regarding its agency-wide contract covering the air traffic controller workforce.[21] In

---

[13] S.Rept. 104-333, at 36 (1996).

[14] *See* H.Rept. 104-848, at 109 (1996).

[15] National Air Traffic Controllers Association v. Federal Service Impasses Panel, 2005 WL 418016 (D.D.C. 2005).

[16] *Id.* at 1-2.

[17] *Id.* at 4.

[18] *Id.*

[19] 437 F.3d 1256 (D.C. Cir. 2006).

[20] *Id.* at 1265.

[21] See FAA Declares Impasse in Controller Talks; Next Stop for Two Sides is Congress, Daily Lab. Rep. (BNA) No. 66, at A-5 (April 6, 2006).

accordance with 49 U.S.C. § 40122(a)(2), the FAA Administrator indicated that the agency would send its last, best offer to Congress.[22] On June 5, 2006, the FAA imposed a new labor contract on NATCA. FAA maintained that the new contract would save the government approximately $1.9 billion over five years through various measures, including the creation of a separate, lower pay scale for new employees.[23]

H.R. 915

Section 601 appears to respond to the events involving NATCA and PASS in 2006. The section would amend 49 U.S.C. § 40122(a)(2) to allow for the involvement of FSIP if the Administrator and a bargaining representative fail to reach agreement under 49 U.S.C. § 40122(a)(1). Under the amended 49 U.S.C. § 40122(a)(2), FSIP would be permitted to assist the parties by ordering binding arbitration by a private arbitration board consisting of three members. Each party would select one arbitrator from a list of not less than 15 arbitrators with federal sector experience provided by the director of the Federal Mediation and Conciliation Service ("FMCS"). The two arbitrators would then select a third arbitrator from the list. If the two arbitrators are unable to agree on the third person, the parties will select the third person by alternately striking names from the list until only one name remains.

The arbitration board would be required to give the parties a full and fair hearing, including the opportunity to present evidence in support of their claims, and an opportunity to present their case in person, by counsel, or by another representative. The arbitration board would be required to render its decision within 90 days of its appointment. The costs of the arbitration would be shared equally by the parties.

In addition, section 601(b) would invalidate any changes that were implemented by the FAA Administrator on and after July 10, 2005, without the agreement of the exclusive bargaining representative. The parties would be governed by their last mutual agreement until a new contract was adopted. Thus, section 601(b) would appear to have the effect of undoing the new contract that was imposed on June 5, 2006.

Sections 602 and 603 would make applicable to the FAA personnel management system additional provisions of Title 5 of the U.S. Code. Section 602, for example, would make applicable to the personnel system 5 U.S.C. §§ 2301 and 2302, which relate to merit systems principles and prohibited personnel practices. Section 603 would make applicable to the personnel system 5 U.S.C. § 5596, which provides for the availability of back pay when there has been an unjustified or unwarranted personnel action. The availability of back pay for personnel actions that occurred prior to the date of enactment of the FAA Reauthorization Act would be limited to cases in which the Merit Systems Protection Board found that the FAA committed an unjustified or unwarranted personnel action, but ruled that the Board did not have the authority to provide a remedy. A petition for review would also have to be filed with the clerk of the Board

---

[22] *Id.* H.R. 5449, a measure introduced by Representative Steven C. LaTourette on May 22, 2006, to repeal 49 U.S.C. § 40122(a)(2), was defeated. The measure was considered under suspension of the rules and required a two-thirds vote to pass. The vote was 271-148. For additional information on the congressional consideration of H.R. 5449, *see FAA Imposes Labor Contract on NATCA Following 60-Day Congressional Review*, Daily Lab. Rep. (BNA) No. 111, at A-10 (June 9, 2006).

[23] FAA Imposes Labor Contract on NATCA Following 60-Day Congressional Review, supra note 22.

within six months after the date of the enactment. The availability of back pay for proceedings pending on or commenced after the date of enactment would not be subject to those conditions.

S. 1451

Section 313 would also amend 49 U.S.C. § 40122(a)(2) to allow for the involvement of FSIP if the Administrator and a bargaining representative fail to reach agreement under 49 U.S.C. § 40122(a)(1). Under the amended 49 U.S.C. § 40122(a)(2), FSIP would be permitted to assist the parties by ordering binding arbitration by a private arbitration board consisting of three members. Each party would select one arbitrator from a list of not less than 15 arbitrators with federal sector experience provided by the director of the FMCS. The two arbitrators would then select a third arbitrator from the list. If the two arbitrators are unable to agree on the third person, the parties will select the third person by alternately striking names from the list until only one name remains.

The arbitration board would be required to give the parties a full and fair hearing, including the opportunity to present evidence in support of their claims, and an opportunity to present their case in person, by counsel, or by another representative. The arbitration board would be required to render its decision within 90 days of its appointment. The costs of the arbitration would be shared equally by the parties.

Unlike H.R. 915, S. 1451 would not invalidate the changes that were implemented by the FAA Administrator on and after July 10, 2005. In addition, S. 1451 does not address the application of 5 U.S.C. §§ 2301, 2302, and 5596 to the FAA personnel management system.

System Capacity

Addressing system congestion and capacity had been a significant issue during FAA reauthorization debate in the 110th Congress. Under the Bush Administration, the FAA made significant legislative and regulatory proposals focused on obtaining the authority to implement market-based approaches to controlling congestion at selected high-density airports. Specifically, it had sought statutory authority to control congestion at certain airports through market-based mechanisms, such as slot auctions and peak-period pricing. In 2008, the Bush Administration sought to impose slot auctions at New York's La Guardia and Kennedy Airports through the regulatory process. This initiative was opposed by many aviation industry groups and by the Port Authority of New York and New Jersey, the airport operator. A December 8, 2008, ruling by the U.S. Court of Appeals put a temporary halt to this initiative.[24]

Indications are that the Obama Administration will not seek to reopen this issue and that it will not be a major issue in its reauthorization proposals. H.R. 915 is silent on these issues except for a provision calling on GAO to study and make recommendations on strategies for relieving congestion at airports and in airspace such as, slots, quotas, and such other remedies as they might identify.

---

[24] *Transportation Weekly.* Appeals Court Puts NY Airport Slot Auctions on Hold. December 18, 2008. p. 2.

Washington Reagan National Airport Slot Controls

The total number of flights that can be handled in a given period of time at Washington Reagan National Airport is set by federal statute (landings and takeoffs are referred to in industry parlance as slots). This system has existed for over two decades, although the statutory limitations on the number of slots available have been modified over that period by congressional action, especially since 2000.

In addition, flights at Reagan National are further restricted by what are known as perimeter rules. These rules, which date to the opening of Dulles Airport in the late 1950s, were designed to move most long-distance airline traffic to the new airport. Again, these perimeter rules have been modified over time. At present, flights of 1,250 miles or less are referred to as being within the perimeter. Prior to congressional action in 2000, all slots for flights arriving or departing Reagan National were required to operate within the perimeter. Since 2000, Reagan National has accommodated additional flights, using newly created slots providing service to destinations outside the perimeter, so-called beyond perimeter slots.

Many Members of Congress and their constituents were long unhappy with the perimeter restrictions, wishing to be able to fly to more distant locations from Reagan National. In 2000, and again in 2003, Congress acceded to this view in a limited fashion, allowing the aforementioned beyond perimeter slots. In the same pieces of legislation, Congress also added additional slots for service within the perimeter, thereby increasing the absolute number of flights allowed per day at the airport.

Certain other Members of Congress, Washington metro area local governments, and local residents living near the airport or in its flight paths have opposed increased traffic at Reagan National for any reason. Although this opposition focuses primarily on the noise impacts of additional traffic, opponents of increased flights have also cited other reasons to hold this view.

In February 2007, the Government Accountability Office (GAO) produced a study that suggested that additional flights could be handled at Reagan National.[25] Although the operator of the airport, the Washington Metropolitan Airports Authority, agreed that additional capacity could be added, it did not support additional slots.

H.R. 915

H.R. 915 provides for an additional 10 beyond perimeter slots, but does so by reducing existing slot allocations at the airport by an equal number.

S. 1451

As reported by the Commerce Committee the bill makes no changes to the existing slot regime at Reagan National. During Committee consideration of the bill, however, a series of amendments that would have changed slot allocations at the airport failed by a very narrow margin. This subject is likely to be revisited during floor consideration of the legislation.

---

[25] U.S. Government Accountability Office. Reagan National Airport: Update on Capacity to Handle Additional Flights and Impact on Other Area Airports. GAO-07-352. Washington, DC. February 2007. 31 p.

Aviation Safety

Both the House and Senate reauthorization bills contains numerous provisions addressing a number of aviation safety issues including whistleblower protections; runway incursions; pilot fatigue; helicopter emergency medical service operations; unmanned aircraft operations; wake turbulence prediction, detection, and avoidance; airline maintenance practices; safety oversight of airline operations; aircrew occupational safety and health; airline pilot training and certification; and concerns over the impact of wind turbine farms on aviation safety.

Investigation of Aviation Safety Concerns by Whistleblowers

A school of thought regarding aviation safety maintains that open communication without fear of reprisal regarding potential safety concerns may improve safety by creating a culture and environment where aviation workers can identify and report unsafe conditions and practices before they lead to mishaps. In line with this view, the Wendell H. Ford Aviation Investment and Reform Act for the 21st Century (AIR-21, P.L. 106-181) established a whistleblower protection program for the airline industry. The act also required the FAA to establish procedures for protecting airlines and their employees from adverse enforcement actions for regulatory violations reported or discovered through voluntary reporting programs, such as the Aviation Safety Action Program (ASAP).

H.R. 915

The bill includes a provision to establish an Aviation Safety Whistleblower Investigation Office within the FAA that would be responsible for looking into complaints, allegations, and information submitted by FAA certificate holders and employees to access whether violations of FAA orders, regulations, standards, or federal laws pertaining to aviation safety may have occurred. The investigation office would be responsible for referring suspected criminal violations to the DOT OIG. The office may issue recommendations to the FAA based on its investigative findings, and would be required to submit annual reports to Congress. The House-passed bill also contains sense of Congress language that whistleblowers at the FAA should be granted the full protection of the law.

S. 1451

Similar to H.R. 915, S. 1451 seeks to establish an Aviation Safety Whistleblower Investigation Office within the FAA.

Runway Safety

Runway incursions—events where aircraft, vehicles, or pedestrians stray onto active runways and pose a collision hazard to landing or departing aircraft—remain a central safety concern. The FAA's major technology initiatives to mitigate runway incursions include the deployment of advanced surface radar capabilities (Airport Surface Detection Equipment, Model X or ASDE-X) and controller alerting to warn of impending incursions (the Airport Movement Area Safety System or AMASS) at busy airports. However, ASDE-X has been scaled back and delayed. Also, the utility of the AMASS system has been questioned by the NTSB because it does not convey warning information directly to pilots, potentially limiting the system's ability to mitigate collisions. The NTSB has recommended that the FAA develop systems that provide direct warnings to pilots. The FAA recently approved the use of electronic flight bags, portable computers for pilot use, with moving maps to improve pilot situation awareness while taxiing. While useful for orienting and navigating in the airport environment, these devices currently do not present information regarding other aircraft and vehicles in the airport environment. To provide direct incursion mitigation tools for pilots, the FAA has been operationally testing the use of runway status lights (RWSLs) to warn taxiing aircraft that it is unsafe to cross an active runway, and final approach runway occupancy signal (FAROS) lights to warn landing aircraft if the runway ahead is occupied. The FAA has not fully evaluated the results of these ongoing operational tests and has not made any decisions regarding the operational deployment of these systems beyond the test phase at this point.

H.R. 915

H.R. 915 contains a provision that would require the FAA to submit a report to Congress detailing its plan to install systems to alert controllers, flight crews, or both of potential runway incursions by December 31, 2009. The FAA would be required to integrate the plan into its annual NextGen Implementation Plan document. As shown in **Table 3**, H.R. 915 also explicitly authorizes, from the amounts authorized for overall Facilities and Equipment (F&E) spending, the amounts specified for runway incursion reduction programs and runway status lights (indicators for taxiing aircraft that a runway is occupied by a landing or departing aircraft and should not be used or crossed). The bill would also require the FAA to develop a strategic plan for runway safety within six months of enactment. The plan would be required to specifically address the effects of expected increases in air traffic on runway safety risk, and include specific goals to improve runway safety; near-term and long-term actions for reducing the number of runway incursions and their severity; a timeline and a list of resources needed for implementing these actions; and details of a continuous process for monitoring progress toward achieving stated runway safety goals. As passed, H.R. 915 also includes a provision expressing the sense of Congress that the FAA should enter into good faith discussions with the city of Santa Monica to achieve runway safety area solutions, to mitigate the effects of possible short landings or runway overruns, that are consistent with FAA design guidelines.

Table 3. Specific Authorizations in H.R. 915 for Runway Incursion Mitigation

($ in millions)

Program	FY2010	FY2011	FY2012
Runway Incursion Reduction Programs	12	12	12
Runway Status Lights	125	100	50

S. 1451

Like H.R. 915, S. 1451 would require the FAA to issue its plan for deploying systems for alerting controllers and flight crews regarding potential runway incursions by December 31, 2009, and integrate it into the annual NextGen Implementation Plan. The Senate would also require the FAA to review all commercial service airports in the United States and initiate action to improve lighting, signage, and runway and taxiway markings. The bill also directs the FAA to develop a process for tracking and investigating operational errors and runway incursions within one year of enactment. The bill also directs the FAA's Air Traffic Organization (ATO) to evaluate the potential contributions of ASDE-X and surface management software to the NextGen initiative. It would also require the FAA to consider available options for expediting certification of Ground Based Augmentation System technology and to develop a plan to utilize such a system at the 35 busiest airports by the end of FY2012.

Pilot Fatigue

Reducing accidents caused by fatigue across all modes of transportation by establishing working hour limits for transportation operators based on fatigue research, circadian rhythms, and sleep and rest requirements has been a longstanding priority of the NTSB. While existing federal regulations include flight time and rest requirements for flight crews that vary depending on the type of commercial flight operation being conducted, these regulations have often been criticized as not adequately reflecting scientific knowledge regarding human fatigue, alertness, and sleep needs. In airline operations, pilot organizations, through collective bargaining, have been able to negotiate schedules that provide longer rest periods than the minimum required under FAA regulations. However, there is still concern that airline pilots' rest periods do not adequately account for the time associated with transportation to and from the airport, and circadian disruption associated with crossing time zones over the course of a trip. However, concern over pilot fatigue tends to be even greater for other commercial operators, besides the airlines, where there are less stringent regulatory requirements for flight time and rest requirements, and fatigue issues are not typically addressed in pilot contracts to the extent that they are covered in contracts between major airlines and their pilots.

H.R. 915

H.R. 915 includes a provision that would task the National Academy of Sciences with completing a study of pilot fatigue, and would require the FAA to implement the recommendations of the CAMI study regarding flight attendant fatigue. H.R. 915 includes an authorization of such sums as may be necessary to carry out this provision. H.R. 915 would also require the FAA to rewrite current flight and duty time regulations for air carrier, commuter airline, and charter pilots to count flight time accumulated conducting non-revenue flight assignments for the operator toward pilot flight and duty time totals.

S. 1451

S. 1451 would require the National Academy of Sciences to carry out a study of pilot fatigue addressing research on fatigue, sleep, and circadian rhythms, related NTSB recommendations, and international standards. The FAA would be required to consider the findings of this study in any rulemaking proceedings regarding flight time limitations and rest requirements. Like H.R. 915, S. 1451 would also require the FAA to initiate a process to implement the CAMI recommendations regarding flight attendant fatigue.

Helicopter Emergency Medical Service Safety

The safety of helicopter emergency medical service (HEMS) operations has been in the spotlight over the past few years in response to increased accidents in this growing industry. The National Transportation Safety Board (NTSB) and other aviation safety experts are advocating the mandatory use of formal flight dispatch procedures and risk management practices among helicopter air ambulance operators as well as mandatory installation of terrain warning systems on HEMS aircraft. The NTSB also found that many air ambulance accidents occur when patients are not on board, such as en route to an accident scene. Present regulations allow air ambulances to operate under a less stringent set of rules with regards to weather minimums and pilot duty times when not carrying patients. However, the NTSB believes that air ambulance flights should operate under more stringent commercial operating rules at all times that medical personnel are carried on board.[26] In 2008, the NTSB added improvements to the safety of emergency medical service flights—including more stringent regulations, flight risk evaluation programs, formal dispatch and flight following procedures providing up-to-date weather information, and the installation of terrain awareness and warning systems (TAWS) on aircraft—to its list of "most wanted" transportation safety improvements.

H.R. 915

Section 313 of the House-passed bill would required the FAA to address HEMS safety through rulemaking. The provision directs the FAA to address dispatch procedures, pilot training standards, and technology and equipment in regulations pertaining to HEMS operators. The FAA would be required to establish training standards in crew resource management (CRM), flight risk evaluation; controlled flight into terrain (CFIT) avoidance; recovery from inadvertent flight into instrument meteorological conditions (IMC); operational control of the pilot in command (PIC); and the use of flight simulators and line oriented flight training (LOFT). The FAA would also be specifically required to address safety technologies, including helicopter TAWS; radar altimeters; and flight data and cockpit voice recorders. Additionally, the FAA would be required to address the use of safety gear including helmets, shoulder harnesses, seatbelts, and fire resistant clothing to improve crash survivability for pilots and medical crews. The provision would require each HEMS operator to establish a flight risk evaluation program, including a checklist for pilots to use in determining whether to accept a mission. HEMS operators with 10 or more helicopters would be required to set up an operations control center. The provision would also require that the FAA enforce commercial operating standards regarding weather minimums and flight and duty time limitations whenever medical personnel are on board, and not just when patients are being transported as is now the case. Also, Section 314 of the bill would require the FAA to complete a study assessing the feasibility of requiring HEMS pilots to use night vision goggles during nighttime operations, and Section 315 of the bill would require the GAO to conduct a study examining safety in the helicopter and fixed-wing air ambulance industry.

S. 1451

S. 1451 would require both fixed-wing and helicopter emergency medical service flights to operate under commercial flight rules specified in 14 CFR Part 135 whenever medical crew are on board, regardless of whether there are patients on board or not. However, operators would be exempt from this requirement if operating under instrument flight rules. While Part 135 flight time and rest requirements and weather minimums would still apply to flights conducted in instrument conditions, they would be exempted from weather reporting requirements at their destination until the FAA determines that destination weather for response sites and other HEMS

---

[26] See CRS Report RL33430, *The Safety of Air Ambulances*, by Bart Elias, and National Transportation Safety Board, *Special Investigation Report on Emergency Medical Service Operations*, NTSB/SIR-06/01.

destinations can be reliably and accurately provided by portable weather measuring and reporting systems.

S. 1451 would also require the FAA to initiate rulemaking within 60 days of enactment to create a standardized checklist of flight risk evaluation factors for HEMS and fixed-wing air ambulances to determine whether a mission should be accepted. It also would require the FAA to initiate rulemaking within 60 days requiring HEMS and fixed-wing air ambulances to implement comprehensive dispatch and flight following procedures. These rulemaking processes must be completed within 18 months. The bill would also require air ambulance operators to submit annual reports to the FAA detailing the number and type of flight requests that are accepted or declined.

S. 1451 also includes a provision requiring the installation and use of TAWS on HEMS and fixed-wing air ambulance aircraft within one year of enactment. The bill would also establish reporting requirements for air ambulance operators to report to the FAA on aircraft in their fleet that perform air ambulance services, and the number of flights and hours flown providing air ambulance services. The FAA, in turn, would be required to submit a report to Congress within 18 months of enactment providing details of the data it obtains regarding the number of air ambulance aircraft, flights, and flights hours flown. The bill would also require the FAA to assess the availability, survivability, size, weight, and cost of cockpit voice recorder and flight data recorder technologies for installation on air ambulance aircraft. Within one year of enactment, the FAA would be required to issue regulations requiring voice communication recorders and flight data recorders on aircraft used for emergency medical service operations. The bill also calls for a GAO study of the HEMS and fixed-wing air ambulance industry.

Incorporating Unmanned Aircraft Operations

Growing interest in the use of unmanned aerial vehicles (UAVs), or unmanned aerial systems (UASs) is spurring considerable debate over how to accommodate these unmanned systems and keep them safely separated from other air traffic. Over the next five to ten years, the FAA anticipates that civilian-use UAVs will rapidly transition to operational status, and users will seek permission to fly UAVs in all airspace throughout the United States in all weather conditions. The FAA and other federal agencies face a wide variety of complex issues related to integrating unmanned aircraft into the National Airspace System (NAS) including reliable technologies for detecting, sensing, and avoiding other aircraft; radio frequency spectrum needs for unmanned aircraft operations; technologies and procedures for systems safety; and training and certification requirements for unmanned aircraft operators.

On February 13, 2007, the FAA issued a notice of policy on unmanned aircraft operations in the national airspace system. That policy states that "no person may operate a UAS in the National Airspace system without specific authority."[27] For military unmanned aircraft and unmanned aircraft operated by federal, state, or local governments, the mechanism for such authority from the FAA is through application for and receipt of a Certificate of Waiver or Authorization (COA). The FAA has issued more than 50 such authorizations over the past two years, mostly to the Department of Defense, but also to other federal agencies such as Customs and Border Protection (CBP), and the National Oceanic and Atmospheric Administration (NOAA). For non-

---

[27] Federal Aviation Administration, "Unmanned Aircraft Operations in the National Airspace System," *Federal Register*, 72(39), February 13, 2007, 6689-6690.

governmental entities seeking authorization to operate unmanned aircraft in the national airspace system, a special airworthiness certificate must be obtained from the FAA. The FAA has indicated that, at present, it is only issuing experimental airworthiness certificates for unmanned aircraft. By being designated as experimental, these vehicles are restricted to sparsely populated areas and away from routes used by manned aircraft. As of February 2007, the FAA had issued five such certificates to civilian organizations for unmanned aircraft research and development, marketing, and training.

However, the FAA is concerned that other civilian users have been operating commercial UAVs under guidelines issued in the early 1980s that were intended to apply only to hobbyists or recreational users of model aircraft. Those guidelines instruct such users to maintain altitudes lower than 400 feet above the ground, select sites away from populated and noise-sensitive areas, give right of way to full-scale aircraft, and advise airport operators and air traffic facilities if operating within three miles of an airport. The FAA statement of policy clarifies that these general guidelines alone are not sufficient for commercial operators of unmanned aircraft, regardless of the size of such aircraft. The FAA did, however, indicate that it has undertaken a safety review to determine whether certain small, slow-moving unmanned aircraft could be safely operated under a similar set of guidelines without requiring a special airworthiness certificate. At present, all such aircraft, except those flown by aircraft model hobbyists, must obtain a special airworthiness certificate as a means of FAA approval for UAV flight operations.

H.R. 915

H.R. 915 includes a provision requiring the FAA to develop a comprehensive plan within nine months of enactment to safely integrate commercial unmanned aircraft systems (UASs) in the national airspace system. The bill further specifies that this integration is to be completed as soon as possible, but not later than September 30, 2012, and authorizes such sums as may be necessary to carry out the implementation plan.

H.R. 915 further requires the Secretary of Transportation to determine if certain UASs can be safely operated in the national airspace system before completion of the integration plan, and establish requirements for safe operation of such aircraft. The bill also requires the Secretary of Transportation to issue guidance within nine months of enactment regarding public unmanned aircraft, such as those operated by federal or state and local entities. The guidance is to expedite certification or authorization of public-use UASs; provide for collaboration with public agencies to allow for incremental expansion of UAS operations as technologies mature; and facilitate the capability of public agencies to develop and use test ranges to fly UASs. The bill also includes a provision directing the FAA, in coordination with other federal agencies, to develop: methods and technologies for assessing risk and preventing design and maintenance related failures of unmanned aircraft systems that could pose risks to other aircraft; a better understanding of human factors issues related to unmanned aircraft systems safety; and dynamic simulation models for assessing the integration of all types of UASs into the national airspace system without causing any degradation of existing levels of safety among all system users. The bill specifies slightly more that $6 million per year for FY2009 through FY2012 for unmanned aircraft system research.

S. 1451

S. 1451 includes a provision requiring the FAA to develop a plan for accelerating the integration of UASs into the NAS within one year of enactment. Under the plan, the FAA would be required to establish a test project examining UAS integration at two test sites by 2012. Under the plan, the FAA would be required to: create a safe, non-exclusionary airspace designation for cooperative manned and unmanned aircraft; establish certification, flight standards, and air traffic requirements for the test sites; dedicate funding for UAS certification, flight standards, and air traffic requirements; encourage the leveraging and coordination of research with NASA and the DoD; address both military and civilian UAS operations; ensure that UAS operations are incorporated into the NextGen system implementation plan; and verify the safety of UAS vehicles and navigational procedures before integrating them into the NAS.

S. 1451 also calls for the FAA to work in conjunction with other Federal agencies to develop technologies and methods to assess the risk and improve the safety of manufactured UASs, and conduct research on human factors aspects of UAS operations. The bill also calls for an assessment by the National Academy of Sciences of UAS technologies and human factors, and directs the FAA to establish three two-year test projects in sparsely populated areas designed to accelerate the safe integration of UASs into the NAS. S. 1451 would also require the FAA to develop a UAS "roadmap," update its policy statement regarding UASs, and issue proposed rulemaking on issuing airworthiness certificates and experimental certificates for UAS systems operated for compensation or hire. The FAA would also be required to assess the potential for using regulations governing ultralight aircraft as the regulatory basis for regulations pertaining to lightweight UASs. The bill would set a deadline of April 30, 2010 for the FAA and other federal agencies to have initiated all rulemaking activity pertaining to UAS design, airworthiness, and operational requirements, and operator certification necessary for integrating UASs into the NAS.

Wake Turbulence Prediction, Detection, and Avoidance

Large transport aircraft generate powerful wingtip vortices that can create turbulence, referred to as wake turbulence, for trailing aircraft. While wake turbulence can be encountered during any phase of flight, it presents a particular constraint on capacity in the airport environment because it is a principal factor in establishing separation standards for landing and departing aircraft. Wake turbulence is therefore a prominent issue with regard to both safety and capacity in the airport environment.

H.R. 915

H.R. 915 authorizes such sums as may be necessary from FY2009 through FY2012 for development and analysis of wake vortex mitigation technologies and systems, including advisory systems. The bill specifies slightly more than $10 million in each of FY2010 through FY2012 specifically for wake turbulence research.

S. 1451

S. 1451 specifies that, within 60 days of enactment, the FAA shall initiate an evaluation of proposals to increase capacity by reducing aircraft spacing, including research on wake vortices. The bill also calls for research on volcanic ash avoidance through a warning and notification system, and research projects on deicing of ice pellets and freezing drizzle, oceanic weather and other hazards, and en route turbulence prediction and detection.

Safety of Airline Maintenance Practices

Concerns over the potential safety implications of a variety of air carrier maintenance practices have been raised by some aviation safety experts and some Members of Congress. Two overarching concerns that have been identified are: the safety of maintenance work outsourced to third-party repair stations, especially repair stations located outside the United States, and the use of non-certificated maintenance providers for routine and extensive repair work and FAA oversight of these non-certificated maintenance providers.

H.R. 915

With regard to airline maintenance, H.R. 915 includes a provision that would restrict the use of non-certified maintenance providers, allowing only airline employees or employees of FAA-certified repair stations to carry out substantial and routine maintenance and complete required inspections of aircraft used in airline service. Air carriers would also be required to provide complete lists of their non-certificated maintenance providers, whose activities would be restricted to non-routine, non-substantial maintenance and repair work under this provision.

The bill also requires the FAA to inspect foreign repair stations that work on U.S. air carrier aircraft or components installed on such aircraft at least two times annually. The FAA would be required to certify to Congress that these inspections have been carried out. The bill would also extend the requirement for drug and alcohol testing programs to safety-critical positions at foreign repair stations working on air carrier aircraft or components. Drug testing programs are already required for safety-critical maintenance personnel working for airlines and repair stations servicing air carrier aircraft within the United States. However, extending these requirements to repair stations in foreign countries may be complicated by specific privacy laws and rights in other countries that may limit the FAA's authority to impose drug and alcohol testing programs that are comparable to existing programs in the United States. Concerns have also been raised that the provision may threaten an aviation safety agreement between the United States and the European Union (EU).[28] Under that agreement, the FAA, the European Aviation Safety Agency (EASA) and aviation safety oversight organizations from EU member countries work collaboratively to certify and inspect repair stations. If the provision is enacted, EU officials have indicated that they may respond by similarly requiring European inspections of repair stations in the United States.[29]

S. 1451

S. 1451 would also require the FAA to carry out inspections of foreign repair stations. The bill requires the FAA to put in place a safety assessment system for all certified repair stations, whether foreign or domestic, within one year of enactment, that is based on the stations type, scope, and complexity of work performed. The system would be required to ensure that foreign

---

[28] Daniel Michaels, "Airline Rule Threatens Pact With EU." *The Wall Street Journal*, May 22, 2009.

[29] Ibid.

repair stations are subject to appropriate inspections based on risk and existing FAA requirements for domestic repair stations. The bill explicitly allows for and directs the FAA to consider maintenance safety and maintenance implementation agreements with foreign civil aviation authorities to oversee foreign repair stations, but stipulates that any such agreements must provide an opportunity for the FAA to conduct independent assessments of overseas repair stations when warranted by safety concerns. Additionally, S. 1451 would require biannual FAA inspections of certified foreign repair stations as well as domestic repair stations in a manner consistent with the terms of international agreements. The FAA would be required to notify congressional oversight committees within 30 days of initiating any formal negotiations with foreign governments regarding maintenance safety or maintenance implementation agreements, and would be required to report annually on improvements in its ability to track where airline maintenance work is performed, and provide a model of maintenance inspector staffing placement needs and maintenance inspector training requirements, and an assessment of the quality of monitoring and surveillance of foreign repair stations by FAA and foreign inspectors.

S. 1451 also addresses drug and alcohol testing for maintenance workers and other safety sensitive positions, including employees of foreign repair stations. S. 1451 would require the DOT and the State Department to request foreign countries to establish international standards for drug and alcohol testing. It would also require the FAA to impose drug and alcohol testing standards on foreign, as well as domestic, repair stations in a manner consistent with the laws of the country in which the repair station is located.

S. 1451 would also require the FAA to regulate non-certificated maintenance providers, stipulating that contract personnel working on airliners must: do so under the supervision of an air carrier or certificated repair station; meet the same standards and requirements as air carrier or certificated repair station personnel; and carry out the work in accordance with the air carrier's maintenance manual.

Safety Oversight of Airline Operations

In addition to concerns over maintenance outsourcing, there has been increasing interest in safety oversight of airline maintenance and flight operations. These issues have largely emerged following the investigation of FAA whistleblower allegations that safety oversight of airline operations were compromised by FAA oversight practices resulting in failures to comply with required safety checks and maintenance actions. The allegations have raised policy questions regarding the FAA's oversight of air carriers, and programs established to encourage airlines and airline employees to come forward with information regarding possible regulatory violations and safety deficiencies.

H.R. 915

Section 336 of the bill seeks to improve the FAA's Voluntary Disclosure Reporting Program (VDRP) that allows airlines to self-disclose safety violations with certain protections established to promote safety rather than seek regulatory enforcement action against the airlines. The language in the bill would require FAA inspectors to verify that air carrier solutions to correct safety violations reported under the VDRP are comprehensive and fully implemented. The bill would also require that inspectors confirm that violations reported by the airline under the VDRP had not been previously discovered by an FAA inspector or previously disclosed by the airline. The bill would require the FAA to establish a process for FAA supervisory inspectors to review and approve VDRP disclosures after they have been initially reviewed by an inspector. The provision also calls for an Inspector General review of the VDRP, including an assessment of whether the program is improving the detection and correction of safety violations and compliance with safety regulations.

The bill also calls for a monthly headquarters level review of the Air Transportation Oversight System (ATOS) database to identify trends in regulatory compliance and corrective actions. The FAA would be required to report quarterly to congressional oversight committees regarding the results of these reviews.

H.R. 915 also contains language that would prohibit former FAA inspectors from working in private sector positions representing air carriers that they had oversight or inspection responsibility over for a period of two after holding such a position at the FAA. The bill would also limit the length of time a principal supervisory inspector would be allowed to oversee the operations of a single air carrier to a term of five years or less.

S. 1451

S. 1451 would similarly require the FAA to take such action as it deems necessary to ensure that, under the VDRP program, FAA inspectors fully evaluate corrective actions proposed by the air carrier before accepting the voluntary disclosure, verify corrective actions are taken within the proposed timeframe, and carry out inspections to assess whether these corrective actions adequately remedy the disclosed problem. The measure would also require a second level supervisory review of all air carrier VDRP submissions to ensure that the problem had not been previously identified by an FAA inspector or disclosed by the airline in the past five years. The Senate bill calls for a GAO study of VDRP, identifying whether it has demonstrated benefits with respect to uncovering problems that may have otherwise gone undetected, and its possible role in reducing violations and improving regulatory compliance.

The Senate bill also directs the FAA to establish a national review team to conduct periodic reviews of FAA air carrier oversight and report annually on its findings to congressional oversight committees, and directs the DOT OIG to monitor and report on the effectiveness of the review teams. The bill also authorizes the FAA to hire an additional 200 safety inspectors. S. 1451 also requires a headquarters level review within the FAA of the ATOS database on a monthly basis to ensure that trends in regulatory compliance issues are adequately identified and corrective actions are taken. The headquarters review team would be required to submit internal FAA reports on a monthly basis as well as quarterly reports to congressional oversight committees. S. 1451 would also require the FAA to develop and implement a plan to ensure safety enforcement consistency within nine months of enactment, and make periodic reviews and updates to that plan as needed.

The Senate bill would require all air carriers to establish a Safety Management System (SMS) that includes an Aviation Safety Action Program (ASAP); a Flight Operations Quality Assurance (FOQA) program; a Line Operational Safety Audit (LOSA) program; and a Flight Crew Fatigue Risk Management program. While many of these aspects of an SMS have been implemented at major airlines, their use is not as prevalent among regional and commuter air carriers. Additionally, the bill would require major airlines to collaborate and conduct operational oversight of their regional and commuter air carrier partners through periodic safety audits; training, maintenance, and inspection programs; and mechanisms for the exchange of safety-related information. In developing regulations for SMS, the FAA would be required to assess the merits and feasibility of using cockpit voice recorder (CVR) data in airline safety oversight practices. Historically, CVR use has been limited to accident investigations. A separate provision of the bill would generally protect ASAP, FOQA and LOSA data from discovery in judicial proceedings, and exempt any such data acquired by the FAA or other federal entity from Freedom of Information Act (FOIA) disclosure requirements. The FAA would, however, be allowed to disclose such information to carry out its safety mission to explain a need for change in policy or regulations, correct a condition that compromises safety, or to carry out a criminal investigation or prosecution. The NTSB would also be allowed to reference such data in issuing its safety recommendations.

S. 1451 would also require the FAA to conduct at least one random, unannounced on-site inspection of regional carriers that have an established contract to provide service with another air carrier to ensure compliance with FAA safety standards. The bill would also prohibit FAA inspectors from accepting positions representing air carriers before the FAA that they were responsible for inspecting and overseeing for a period of three years after leaving the FAA.

Occupational Safety and Health

The FAA, under its broad authority and responsibility for regulating aviation safety, has asserted its responsibility for regulating matters pertaining to the occupational safety and health of aircraft crewmembers including pilots and flight attendants.[30] In August 2000, the FAA entered into a Memorandum of Understanding (MOU) with the Occupational Safety and Health Administration (OSHA) to determine whether certain OSHA requirements could be applied to working conditions in the airline environment without compromising aviation safety and in a manner that would maintain the FAA's "complete and exclusive jurisdiction over aviation safety."[31] OSHA's role in airline occupational safety, under this arrangement, remains strictly advisory in nature. Under the MOU, the FAA and OSHA established a joint Aviation Safety and Health Team. That team sought to identify occupational hazards in the airline setting and assess the feasibility of complying with OSHA requirements to mitigate those hazards. The team finalized an action plan in June 2002 for establishing voluntary Aviation Safety and Health Partnership (ASHP) programs with air carriers, but work has not been completed to implement these initiatives.

H.R. 915

H.R. 915 would establish new statutory requirements for occupational safety and health standards for flight attendants onboard aircraft. The FAA, in consultation with OSHA, would be required to issue and enforce standards and regulations for air carriers within three years of enactment "to provide for an environment in the cabin ... that is free from hazards that could cause physical harm to a flight attendant." The FAA would be specifically required to conduct rulemaking to address record keeping; blood-borne pathogens; noise; sanitation; hazard communication; anti-discrimination; access to employee exposure and medical records; and setting a standard for aircraft cabin temperature. The FAA would also be required to employ qualified Cabin Occupational Safety and Health Inspectors to oversee regulatory compliance among air carriers.

---

[30] See Federal Aviation Administration, "Occupational Safety or Health Standards for Aircraft Crewmembers," *Federal Register, 75-17859*, July 9, 1975.

[31] p. 3.

S. 1451

S. 1451 would require the FAA, in consultation with OSHA, to establish milestones for completing the work begun under the August 2000 MOU. The FAA would also be required to initiate development of a policy statement setting forth circumstances under which OSHA requirements may be applied to crewmembers onboard an aircraft. The policy statement would be required within 18 months of enactment and would establish a coordinating body, similar to the Aviation Safety and Health Joint Team established under the August 2000 MOU. The coordinating body would be responsible for examining the applicability of current and future OSHA regulations on aircraft, make recommendations regarding the training of FAA inspectors, and make recommendations regarding inspection and enforcement of safety and health standards.

S. 1451 also includes a provision that would require flight attendants serving on domestic flights and flights to and from the United States to demonstrate proficiency in English sufficient to provide direction to and answer questions from English speakers; to write up incident reports, log entries, and statements; and to carry out written and oral instructions regarding the proper performance of their duties.

Airline Pilot Training and Certification

The February 12, 2009, crash of a regional airline turboprop near Buffalo, NY, has raised policy questions about the selection and training of pilots at regional airlines, particularly pilots hired from civilian flight schools. The investigation has also raised questions about pilot records, airline access to these records to assess new hires, and remedial actions taken when pilots repeatedly fail to demonstrate required proficiency during flight evaluations.

H.R. 915

Section 830 of the House-passed bill would require the GAO to conduct a study of commercial airline pilot training and certification programs. The study would examine training hour requirements, training on new technologies introduced in the cockpit, remedial actions for repeated unsatisfactory evaluations (check-rides), and training on stall warning systems. The study would also be required to assess the disclosure requirements for pilot job applicants and the ability of airlines to verify information provided by applicants. The GAO would be required to examine both FAA and international standards regarding commercial airline pilot training and certification programs.

S. 1451

The Senate bill would require the FAA to establish and maintain a centralized database of pilot employment, training, and testing records. The database would be required to include information on pilot certifications, medical certifications, type ratings, and any limitations placed on a pilot. The database would also be required to include information regarding any failed attempt to pass a practical test for a pilot certificate or rating, and summaries of any legal enforcement actions taken by the FAA against the pilot so long as such actions were not subsequently overturned. The database would also be required to include records from air carriers and other entities, such as charter operators or flight schools, that employed an individual as a civilian pilot or the pilot of a public aircraft pertaining to the individuals performance as a pilot, training, qualifications, proficiency, and professional competence. Such records are to include comments made by check airman; any disciplinary action taken against the pilot that was not subsequently overturned; and documentation of any release from employment, resignation, termination, or disqualification with respect to employment. The centralized database is also to include National Driver Register (NDR) records from each state. Pilots would have the right to review their information and correct any inaccuracies in the database, and airlines must take steps to protect the privacy and confidentiality of any records it obtains for the purpose of making hiring decisions. The FAA would be required to assess any developments in the aviation industry that may warrant changes to the contents of the records maintained in the central database, and report to Congress on its recommendations for change or its rationale for retaining the database as is. Prior to beginning service as a pilot for an airline, the air carrier would be required to request and review the pilot's complete records. To expedite the records review process, the FAA may designate certain air carrier representatives to have electronic access to these records solely for the purposes of making hiring decisions.

S. 1451 would also require the FAA to reevaluate flight crew training regulations and incorporate industry best practices regarding training protocols, methods, and procedures. The FAA would also be required to reevaluate the minimum requirements for obtaining commercial pilot and air transport pilot (ATP) certificates and type certification required to transition to different aircraft. The bill would also require the FAA to issue a final rule based on its proposed changes to airline training programs for flight crews and dispatchers. It would also require the FAA to submit a plan to Congress for stepping up oversight of FAA-certificated flight training schools to ensure that these schools are meeting the minimum curriculum and course of study requirements established by the FAA, and to conduct on-site inspections of each flight training school at least once every two years.

Addressing Safety Concerns Over Wind Turbines

With growing interest in the deployment of renewable energy technologies, there has been increasing concern over the potential impacts of wind turbine farms used for electric power generation on aviation safety. In particular, concerns have been raised that tall wind turbines can be a hazard to low-flying aircraft, and the motion of their fan blades may interfere with FAA surveillance radars that monitor air traffic. Both the FAA and the U.S. Air Force have been studying the issue of radar interference, and have been working with local authorities and power companies on a case-by-case basis to address concerns and identify suitable sites for wind turbine farms that will not interfere with radars or air traffic patterns. However, advocates for renewable energy regard these concerns over aviation safety as a potential impediment to expeditious approval and construction of wind turbine farms.

H.R. 915

H.R. 915, as agreed to by the House, would require the FAA to conduct a study addressing the impact of renewable energy technologies, and planning for the installation of such technologies, on FAA radar signals. The provision would also require the FAA to establish an administrative process for relocating FAA radars, when appropriate and deploying alternative solutions as necessary to accommodate the construction of wind turbine farms and other renewable energy technologies. The bill also includes a provision that would require the FAA to study wind turbine lighting systems that warn pilots regarding the presence of tall obstructions. The study would specifically require the FAA to examine the effect of the lights on residential areas, and the feasibility, potential energy savings, and safety issues associated with alternative lighting options.

S. 1451

S. 1451 would require the FAA to develop an inventory of leases for critical FAA facilities, including a list of such facilities located in or near areas suitable for the construction of wind farms, as determined by the Department of Energy, and provide congressional oversight committees with its findings, conclusions, and recommendations. The bill also calls for a GAO study of the potential impact of wind farms on the NAS, including NextGen technologies and aids to navigation. The GAO would be required to assess necessary resources to mitigate obstructions to navigation attributable to wind farms, improvements to current FAA approaches to resolving potential conflicts between navigational aids and wind farms, with an emphasis on early involvement in the planning of wind farm projects. The GAO would also be required to develop a matrix indicating how close wind farms could be placed to navigational aids, and the number of wind turbines that could be placed in the vicinity of such facilities. Based on the GAO findings, the FAA would be required to publish guidelines for the construction and location of wind farms specifying height and density limits, and other design requirements or recommendations, for zones around FAA navigational facilities.

Environmental and Energy Issues

Aviation and airport operations have air quality, water quality, waste, and community noise impacts.[32] Within the context of FAA reauthorization, options for researching and mitigating these impacts are being considered. To address issues associated with environmental impacts, and to assist airport operators with complying with local, state, and federal regulations related to those impacts, H.R. 915 and S. 1451 include provisions that would:

- Require research into technology or processes that would reduce noise, air emissions, water quality impacts, and energy use;

- Provide grants for programs or projects intended to mitigate or minimize regulated environmental impacts;

- Specify changes applicable to airport environmental compliance requirements; and

- Specify requirements to address airport and aircraft air and noise emission issues (including modifications to the Air Tour Management Program).

In addition to the categories listed above, H.R. 915 (§ 511) would require the FAA, to the maximum extent possible, to implement "sustainable practices" in the construction and major renovation of air traffic control facilities in order to reduce energy use and improve environmental performance at those facilities. Also, under § 202, the House proposal specifies certain environmental-related responsibilities of the JPDO. Included is a directive to establish specific quantitative goals for, among other factors, the environmental impacts of each phase of NextGen Air Transportation System. In establishing the environmental goals, the FAA is required to take into account noise pollution reduction concerns of affected communities, to the greatest extent practicable.

---

[32] For additional background see CRS Report RL33949, *Environmental Impacts of Airport Operations, Maintenance, and Expansion*, by Linda Luther.

Both the House and Senate proposals include provisions intended to reduce waste generation at airports (House, § 132 "Solid Waste Recycling Plans," Senate, § 714, "Recycling Plans for Airports"). Each proposal would amend the definition of "airport planning"[33] to include planning to minimize the generation airport solid waste in a manner that is consistent with applicable state and local recycling laws. Both proposals would also amend the list of conditions under which an airport improvement grant application may be approved.[34] Under those conditions, airports required to have an airport master plan must address (in the master plan) factors such as the feasibility of solid waste recycling at the airport and minimizing the generation of solid waste at the airport.

Environmental-Related Research Funding and Requirements

H.R. 915

Under § 907, H.R. 915 would permanently authorize the Airport Cooperative Research Program (ACRP).[35] Of funding amounts made available under § 102 ("Airport Planning and Development and Noise Compatibility Planning and Programs"), $15 million for each of the FYs 2010 through 2012 may be used for carrying out the ACRP. Further, under § 104 ("Research, Engineering, and Development"), [36] additional environmental-related funding authorizations for FY2010 through FY2012 include approximately $91.8 million for "environment and energy" projects and approximately $60 million for "NextGen—Environmental Research—Aircraft technologies, fuels, and metrics."

H.R. 915 would require FAA, in coordination with NASA, to enter into a cooperative agreement with another institution or consortium to develop Continuous Low Energy, Emissions and Noise (CLEEN) engine and airframe technology over the next ten years (§ 507). The House proposal requires that, by September 30, 2016, the following performance objectives shall be established:

- Development of aircraft technology that reduces fuel burn by 33% compared to current technology, reducing energy consumption and greenhouse gas emissions.

- Development of engine technology that reduces nitrogen oxide emissions during landing and takeoff.

- Development of aircraft technology that reduces noise levels by 32 Effective Perceived Noise Level in Decibels cumulative, relative to Stage 4 standards.

- Determination of the feasibility of the use of alternative fuels in aircraft systems, including successful demonstration and quantification of the benefits of such fuels.

---

[33] 49 U.S.C. § 47102(5).

[34] 49 U.S.C. § 47106(a).

[35] The ACRP was authorized as a four-year pilot program under Vision 100 (49. U.S.C. § 44511(f)). Funds for the program are authorized under the Airport and Airway Trust Fund Authorizations, under the Airport Planning and Development and Noise Compatibility Planning and Programs.

[36] Projects specified under § 104 of H.R. 915 amend the Research and Development section of the Airport and Airway Trust Fund Authorizations at 49 U.S.C. § 48102.

- Determination of the extent to which new engine and aircraft technologies may be used to retrofit or re-engine aircraft to increase the integration of retrofitted and re-engined aircraft into the commercial fleet.

Funding for the program from FY2010 through FY2012, under the Airport and Airway Trust Fund Authorization, would be $108 million.

Under Title IX—Federal Aviation Research and Development, H.R. 915 includes the following additional environmental-related research and development requirements (except where noted, the bill does not specifically authorize funds for this research):

- **Interagency research initiative on the impact of aviation on the climate (§ 903)**—directs the FAA Administrator, in coordination with NASA and the U.S. Global Climate Change Science Program, to establish a research initiative to assess the impact of aviation on climate and to evaluate approaches to mitigate that impact.

- **Aviation gas research and development program (§ 910)**—would require the FAA, in coordination with NASA, to continue to study technologies that would allow the use of unleaded gasoline in piston-engine aircraft (currently, piston-engine aircraft—mostly general aviation aircraft—use leaded gasoline). The bill would authorize $750,000 to be appropriated for each of the FYs 2010 through 2012.

- **Research reviews and assessments (§ 911)**—would require the FAA to contract with the National Research Council to assess the adequacy of FAA's energy- and environment-related research programs. Among other requirements, the review must assess whether such FAA research programs are properly coordinated with NASA, the National Oceanic and Atmospheric Administration (NOAA), and other relevant agencies.

- **Research program on alternative jet fuel technology for civil aircraft (§ 913)**—would establish a research program to conduct research into the development of jet fuels from alternative sources such as coal, natural gas, biomass, ethanol, butanol, and hydrogen. Funds for the program would be authorized from the Airport and Airway Trust Fund.

S. 1451

The Senate proposal would also permanently authorize the Airport Cooperative Research Program (§ 601). It would authorize $15 million to be appropriated for the program for FYs 2010 and 2011. The Senate proposal also specifies that not less than $5 million shall be used for "research activities related to the airport environment, including reduction of community exposure to civil aircraft noise, reduction of civil aviation emissions, or addressing water quality issues."

Similar to § 507 of the House proposal, § 602 of the Senate proposal ("Reduction of Noise, Emissions, and Energy Consumption From Civilian Aircraft") would establish a research program related to reducing civilian aircraft source noise and emissions through grants or other measures authorized under the Airport and Airways Trust Fund Authorizations.

The program would include participation of educational and research institutions or private sector entities that have existing facilities and experience developing and testing noise, emissions and energy reduction engine and aircraft technology, and developing alternative fuels. Similar to the House proposal, the Senate proposal would establish a "Consortium for Aviation Noise, Emissions, and Energy Technology Research" to perform research in coordination with NASA and other relevant agencies. The five performance objectives of the research programs specified in the Senate proposal are essentially identical to the performance objectives specified in the House proposal.

Additional environmental-related research and development requirements specified under Title VI—Aviation Research of S. 1451 include the following (the bill does not specifically authorize funds for this research):

- **Production of Clean Coal Fuel Technology for Civilian Aircraft (§ 603)**— would establish a research program related to developing jet fuel from clean coal through grants or other measures. The program would be required to include participation by educational and research institutions that have existing facilities and experience in the development and deployment of technology that processes coal to aviation fuel. Further, the FAA would be required to designate such an educational or research institution as a "Center of Excellence for Coal-to-Jet-Fuel Research."

- **Pilot Program for Zero Emission Airport Vehicles (§ 609)**—would establish a pilot program under which certain public-use airports may use funds[37] to acquire and operate zero emission vehicles. The federal share of the costs of a project carried out under the program would be 50%.

- **Reduction of Emissions from Airport Power Sources (§ 610)**—would amend the "Airport ground support equipment emissions retrofit pilot program"[38] to establish a program that under which certain airports would be encouraged to assess their energy requirements, including heating and cooling, base load, back-up power, and power for on-road airport vehicles and ground support equipment, to identify opportunities to reduce harmful emissions, and to increase energy efficiency at the airport. Grants for such an assessment would be available under the Airport and Airway Trust Fund Authorizations.[39]

- **Research Improvement for Aircraft (§ 216)**–would amend "Facility, Personnel, and Research" requirements with regard to "improved aircraft, aircraft engines, propellers, and appliances"[40] to require the Administrator to conduct or supervise research to "support programs designed to reduce gases and particulates emitted."

---

[37] Available under the Airport Improvement requirements at 49 U.S.C. § 47117 or the airport planning and development and noise compatibility planning and programs of the Airport and Airway Trust Fund Authorizations at 49 U.S.C. § 48103.

[38] 49 U.S.C. § 47140.

[39] 49 U.S.C. § 48103.

[40] 49 U.S.C. § 44504(a).

Mitigation Grants

H.R. 915

Section 509 of the House proposal would establish a trial program to provide grants for up to six environmental mitigation demonstration projects. Eligible projects would include those that would reduce or mitigate aviation impacts on noise, air quality, or water quality in the vicinity of the airport. The federal share of the projects would be 50% of the project costs, up to $2.5 million, and would be apportioned under the AIP.

S. 1451

Section 213 of the Senate proposal is similar to the House proposal.

Grants and Procedural Changes to Assist with Environmental Compliance

Both the House and Senate bills include almost identical proposals that would amend the state block program, address methods of expediting compliance with the National Environmental Policy Act (NEPA), and amend certain noise compatibility program requirements.

H.R. 915

The House proposal would amend the state block grant program[41] to specify that federal, state, and local environmental requirements, including the National Environmental Policy Act (NEPA, 42 U.S.C. § 4321 *et seq.*),[42] would apply to the program (§ 502). The proposal specifies that any federal agency that must grant any approval (i.e., permit or license) to a state must consult with that state during the approval process. Further, the federal agency would be required to use any state-prepared environmental analysis associated with that approval.

Under § 503, the House bill would amend current requirements that allow FAA to accept funds from an airport sponsor to hire additional staff or obtain the services of consultants to expedite the processing, review, and completion of environmental activities associated with an airport development project.[43] The proposal would allow FAA to accept funds to hire additional staff to: conduct "special environmental studies" related to a federally funded airport project; conduct studies or reviews to support noise compatibility measures approved under the Part 150[44]

---

[41] 49 U.S.C. § 47128.

[42] Among other provisions, NEPA requires airport operators to consider the environmental impact of any proposed action that may require federal funding or approvals. It also requires them to look at all reasonable alternatives to meet a given project's purpose and need, before final decisions are made. For more information, see FAA's "NEPA Implementing Instructions for Airport Projects," Order 5050.4B, April 28, 2006, available online at http://www.faa.gov/airports_airtraffic/airports/resources/publications/orders/environmental_5050_4/.

[43] 49 U.S.C. § 47173.

[44] Airport Noise Compatibility Planning requirements are specified under 14 C.F.R. Part 150 and are, hence, commonly referred to as "Part 150" requirements.

requirements; or conduct studies or reviews to support environmental mitigation specified in a project's final decision and delineated at the completion of the NEPA process.

Also with regard to environmental compliance assistance, the House proposal (§ 504) would amend the existing noise compatibility program requirements[45] to allow grants to airport operators to assist them in completing environmental review[46] requirements for proposals to implement flight procedures. Further, the proposal would allow a project sponsor to provide FAA with funds to hire additional staff as necessary to expedite completion of the environmental review necessary to implement flight procedures.

S. 1451

Provisions of §§ 209 ("State Block Grant Program"), 210 ("Airport Funding of Special Studies or Reviews"), and 210 ("Grant Eligibility for Assessment of Flight Procedures") of the Senate proposal are essentially identical to §§ 502, 503, and 504, respectively, of the House proposal.

Requirements to Address Aircraft and Airport Air Emissions and Noise

In 1990, Congress mandated a phase out of non-Stage 3 aircraft over 75,000 pounds by December 31, 1999.[47] This has allowed Stage 1 and Stage 2 aircraft *under* 75,000 pounds, primarily corporate and private-use aircraft, to continue to operate. In 2006, non-Stage 3 aircraft represented a relatively small number of all operational turbojet aircraft under 75,000 pounds (approximately 1,330 or 13%). However, at some airports, particularly smaller commercial and general aviation airports, their use makes a disproportionate contribution to noise exposure contours. For example, the Massachusetts Port Authority (Massport) reported that at the L.G. Hanscom Field in Bedford, MA, non-Stage 3 aircraft accounted for less than one percent of the airport's annual traffic in 2005, yet were responsible for 23 percent of the noise energy produced by civil aircraft.[48] Also, some airport operators have reported that between 50 and 80% of noise complaints lodged with the airport have been related to non-Stage 3 aircraft.[49] As a result, several airports have sought to ban or restrict access to such aircraft. Those efforts have generally been prohibited by FAA. Both the House and Senate proposals include provisions to address issues associate Stage 1 and 2 aircraft.

---

[45] 49 U.S.C. § 47504.

[46] Generally, "environmental review" requirements refer to environmental review requirements specified under the NEPA regulations. However, they may apply more broadly to any review, study, or analysis required by any other environmental law applicable to a given project.

[47] Airport Noise and Capacity Act of 1990 (P.L. 101-508).

[48] Massport December 19, 2006, press release: "Massport Endorses Congressional Efforts To Ban Stage 2 Aircraft; Less than one percent of Hanscom Field's traffic accounts for 23 percent of aircraft noise," at http://www.massport.com/about/press06/press_news_hanst.html.

[49] See the statement of Mr. Robert L. Bogan, Deputy Director of the Morristown Municipal Airport on behalf of "The Sound Initiative," presented to the House Transportation and Infrastructure Committee's Subcommittee on Aviation hearing on "The FAA's Airport Improvement Program," March 28, 2007, at http://transportation.house.gov/hearings/hearingdetail.aspx?NewsID=59.

H.R. 915

Section 508 of the House proposal would prohibit the operation of aircraft under 75,000 pounds, with certain exceptions, not complying with Stage 3 noise levels. The prohibition would take effect January 1, 2014.

The following sections of the House proposal also deal with issues associated with airport and aircraft noise or air emissions:

- **Determination of Fair Market Value of Residential Properties (§ 505)**—specifies that, in approving the use of noise compatibility funds for the acquisition of residential real property, the FAA must ensure that the property appraisal disregards any decrease or increase in the fair market value of the real property caused by the project for which the property is to be acquired.

- **Soundproofing of Residences (§ 506)**—amends the list of potential projects that may receive grant funding for "Soundproofing and Acquisition of Certain Residential Buildings and Properties" under Aviation Noise Compatibility Programs.[50] This section would also require FAA to establish certain grant criteria that must be met before a grant can be awarded.

- **Aircraft Departure Queue Management Pilot Program (§ 510)**—funds a pilot program at five public-use airports that would be required to develop and test new air traffic flow management technologies to better manage the flow of aircraft on the ground and reduce ground holds and idling times for aircraft to decrease emissions and increase fuel savings. Not more than $5 million may be expended under the trial program at any single public-use airport. Also, a report to Congress on the effectiveness and potential benefits of the program must be made not later than three years after enactment of the program.

- **Regulatory Responsibility for Aircraft Engine Noise and Emissions Standards (§ 512)**—directs the FAA, in consultation with the Environmental Protection Agency (EPA), to make arrangements with the National Academy of Public Administration (or another qualified entity) to review whether it is desirable to locate the regulatory responsibilities regarding the establishment of engine noise and air emission standards within one of the agencies (i.e., FAA or EPA). The review would be required to consider, among other factors, the degree to which those standards could be evaluated and addressed in an integrated manner.

- **Sense of Congress (§ 514)**—specifies the sense of the Congress with respect to the European Union (EU) directive extending the EU's emission trading proposal to international civil aviation. The bill specifies that, by not working through the International Civil Aviation Organization in a consensus-based fashion, the EU directive is inconsistent with the Convention on International Civil Aviation; and that it is antithetical to building international cooperation to address greenhouse gas emissions from aircraft.

---

[50] 49 U.S.C. § 47504(c)(2)(D).

- **Airport Noise Compatibility Planning Study, Port Authority of New York and New Jersey (§ 515)**—specifies that it is the sense of the House that the Port Authority of New York and New Jersey undertake an airport noise compatibility planning study[51]—with particular attention to the impact of noise on affected neighborhoods, including homes, businesses, and places of worship surrounding LaGuardia Airport and JFK Airport.

- **GAO Study on Compliance With FAA Record of Decision (§ 516)**—directs GAO to determine whether the FAA and the Massachusetts Port Authority are complying with the requirements of the FAA's August 2, 2002 record of decision regarding the Boston Airport Noise Study.

- **Westchester County Airport, New York (§ 517)**—requires FAA to conduct a rulemaking proceeding to determine whether Westchester County Airport should be authorized to limit aircraft operations between the hours of 12 a.m. and 6:30 a.m.

- **Aviation Noise Complaints (§ 518)**—requires that each owner or operator of a large hub airport post to the airport's website, a telephone number to receive aviation noise complaints related to the airport. Annually after implementation, any owner or operator that receives one or more complaints, must submit a report to the Administrator regarding the number of complaints received and a summary of the nature of the complaints. Also, FAA must make that information available to the public by print and electronic means.

S. 1451

The Senate proposal also proposes to phase out Stage 1 and 2 aircraft. Provisions under § 710 of the S. 1451 are essentially identical to § 508 of H.R. 915, except that the Senate proposal would allow airport operators to opt out of the prohibition under certain conditions. The provisions in the Senate proposal would take effect five years after enactment of the law.

Under § 104, S. 1451 amends the Airport and Airway Trust Fund Authorizations to include $8.1 billion for airport planning and development and noise compatibility planning and programs for FYs 2010 and 2011.

Section 712 of S. 1451 would create a pilot program for the redevelopment of property purchased with noise mitigation funds or passenger facility charge funds, to encourage airport-compatible land uses. The trial program would involve up to four airport operators that have submitted a noise compatibility program to FAA. Provisions in this section would also amend the list of allowable noise compatibility measures[52] to include land use planning that will prevent the introduction of additional incompatible land uses.

---

[51] Pursuant to Airport Noise Compatibility Planning requirements under 14 C.F.R. 150.

[52] 49 U.S.C. 47504(a)(2).

The Air Tour Management Program

The National Parks Air Tour Management Act of 2000 (Title VIII, P.L. 106-181, hereinafter "Air Tour Act") regulates commercial air tours over most units of the National Park System. It requires the FAA and the National Park Service (NPS) to create management plans for air tours at individual park units and within a half-mile of their boundaries. The purpose of a plan is to mitigate or prevent any significant adverse impacts of commercial air tours to natural and cultural resources, visitor experiences, and adjacent tribal lands.

The Air Tour Act final rule[53] requires air tour operators to apply for authority to fly over national park and adjacent tribal lands. The FAA received applications for commercial air tours over 106 of the 391 park units, and has granted interim operating authority to all applicants. An application triggers development of an Air Tour Management Plan (ATMP) by the FAA and NPS for each unit where there is no existing plan.[54] Development of an ATMP requires an environmental analysis under the National Environmental Policy Act of 1969 (NEPA, 42 U.S.C. §§4321-4370f). The FAA and NPS currently are developing their first ATMPs for several park units. A January 2006 Government Accountability Office (GAO) report concluded that the delay in implementing the Air Tour Act has limited the ability of tour operators to make major business decisions. GAO further concluded that Congress may wish to consider amending the Air Tour Act to give the agencies discretion in determining which park units may need ATMPs.[55]

H.R. 915

H.R. 915 includes provisions affecting commercial air tours over park units (codified in 49 U.S.C. §40128) that seek to expedite and streamline agency actions, in part due to the difficulty in completing ATMPs. One change would allow that in lieu of an ATMP, the NPS Director and FAA Administrator (hereinafter in this section "the Administrator") could enter into a voluntary agreement with a commercial air tour operator that would govern commercial air tours over a park unit. An agreement would address protection of park resources and visitor use of the park in the context of aviation safety and the air traffic control system. It would be prepared with an opportunity for public review and consultation, and implemented "without further administrative or environmental process" (e.g., NEPA) beyond that described in the legislation. The NPS and FAA heads could terminate a voluntary agreement if it did not adequately protect park resources, visitor experiences, aviation safety, or the national aviation system. A second change would exempt park units with 50 or fewer annual air tour flights from the development of an ATMP or voluntary agreement and other requirements covering air tour operations over park units. However, the NPS Director is to withdraw the exemption for any park unit for which an ATMP or voluntary agreement would be necessary to protect park resources and values or park visitor use and enjoyment. Other provisions in the bill could provide more interim operating authority "without further environmental review" beyond that described, because interim conditions have prevailed for longer than had been anticipated. Still other provisions would require commercial air tour operators to report to the agencies on their operations. Some of the changes in H.R. 915

---

[53] 67 *Fed. Reg.* 65661 (October 25, 2002).

[54] The FAA provides ATMP information on its website at http://www.faa.gov/about/office_org/headquarters_offices/arc/programs/air_tour_management_plan/more_tour_management_plan.cfm.

[55] The report, including information on agency actions on GAO recommendations, is available on the GAO website at http://www.gao.gov/new.items/d06263.pdf.

could be opposed as lessening public participation in the decision making process and/or weakening environmental analysis of agency decisions.

S. 1451

S. 1451 also contains provisions pertaining to commercial air tours over park units. It would allow "appropriate representatives of the national park" and a commercial air tour operator to develop a voluntary agreement to govern air tours over a national park unit. Unlike the House bill, it does not exempt parks with 50 or fewer annual flights from the requirement to develop an ATMP or a voluntary agreement. It also would allow the agencies to modify interim operating authority "without further environmental process." Other provisions would allow an air tour operator that obtains operating authority for commercial air tours to transfer that authority to another air tour operator. The bill also establishes reporting requirements for commercial air tour operators, but would rescind the operating authority of a commercial air tour operator that does not report and require the Inspector General of the Department of Transportation to audit the reports. Other provisions would authorize the Secretary of the Interior to assess a fee on commercial air tour operators, and the Administrator is to revoke the operating authority of a tour operator that does not pay the fee. The Secretary is to consider the cost of developing ATMPs in setting the fee.

Airline Industry Issues

A wide array of aviation industry issues are being considered in the context of FAA reauthorization. Modifications to the Essential Air Service (EAS) program that provides subsidy incentives to airlines for servicing small, rural, or otherwise isolated communities are contentious issues in every reauthorization debate. H.R. 915 seeks increased funding and other program enhancements. Also, H.R. 915 seeks to clarify foreign ownership issues related to operational control of U.S. flag airlines, a central issue for potentially expanding "Open Skies" arrangements with the European Union (EU) in the future. Also, H.R. 915 includes a provision addressing union issues among express carriers in language that would limit applicability of the Railway Labor Act (RLA) to employees engaged in airline operations, placing other employees under the terms of the National Labor Relations Act (NLRA). Another ongoing issue is the consideration of legislation regarding airline passenger rights, particularly with respect to flights that experience extreme delays or flights that are chronically late. These issues are further discussed below.

The Essential Air Service Program

The Essential Air Service Program (EAS) is a DOT-managed program that subsidizes air carrier service to small and isolated communities. Over time the scope of the EAS program has been modified by statute and regulation. The program, however, remains popular, especially in rural areas of the Nation.

The EAS program provides subsidies to air carriers for providing service between selected small communities and hub airports. The program was originally established in 1978 as part of airline deregulation to ensure a minimum level of air service to smaller communities that might otherwise lose service because of economic factors.

During its years in office, the George W. Bush Administration routinely suggested limiting annual EAS funding to $50 million and requiring local cost-sharing as a condition for a community's continued participation in the program. The program nonetheless has grown as Congress has provided additional funding for EAS.

Vision 100 included several mechanisms and incentives designed to move communities out of the standard EAS program. Communities have not sought to participate in these incentive regimes, however, suggesting that the incentives themselves may need to be reconsidered if they are to be effective. Vision 100 also included a somewhat controversial provision that created a trial program that would have required community financial participation as a condition for continued access to EAS funding in some instances. Each annual appropriations bill since passage of Vision 100, however, has prevented the use of any appropriated funds to implement the cost-sharing trial program.

H.R. 915

As passed by the House the bill makes several modifications to the EAS program. Most notable is a significant increase in funding. The bill reserves $50 million annually in overflight fee collections for the EAS program and provides for an overall authorization of $77 million. The bill also makes $150 million available annually for appropriation from the airport and airway trust fund Funds available from overflight fee collections in excess of $50 million for EAS, are split between EAS and the Small Community Air Service Program.

H.R. 915 encourages the use of financial incentives and long term contracts as part of the EAS program. In light of problems experienced by the program in 2008, the bill allows EAS subsidy caps to be adjusted to account for rapid fluctuations in fuel prices. The bill also provides for rapid adjustment to EAS subsidies to account for other rapid cost increases that if not addressed might jeopardize the continuation of service. H.R. 915 reauthorizes the somewhat related, but separate, Small Community Air Service program for the life of the legislation.

S. 1451

The Senate bill also modifies the EAS program. The bill raises funding in the same manner as that found in H.R. 915, except that fund collected from oversight fees in excess of $50 million are reserved solely for EAS activities. The bill adds two new provisions to the EAS program. The first of these, allows State and local governments, working with the Secretary, to maintain service at locations where the existing per passenger subsidy cap would be exceeded, providing that some party (government and/or private) was willing to subsidize the additional cost of the service. The second new provision allows state/local governments to designate a preferred air carrier for EAS service, which would not necessarily be the lowest bidder for the service.

The bill also provides for the establishment of an Office of Rural Aviation within DOT with several duties, including the development of model four year EAS contracts. S. 1451 would also allow for longer term service contracts and includes a provision that disregards fuel cost subsides in the calculation of subsidy caps.

Airline Ownership

Existing law specifically limits non-U.S. ownership of United States certificated airlines.[56] These provisions are viewed by many as exclusionary, preventing all but limited foreign investment in the U.S. domestic airline industry, and absolutely preventing any real non-U.S. control over an airline's business decisions. These laws are seen by proponents of the industry's internationalization as major barriers to a fully open international aviation market. A recent initiative by the Bush Administration to lift some of the existing ownership and control restrictions through the regulatory process was opposed by Congress and ultimately abandoned by the Bush Administration. A recently concluded "Open Skies" agreement with the European Union (EU) suggests that the discussion about airline ownership and control issues could be reopened at some later date.

H.R. 915

H.R. 915 addresses this issue by including language to be inserted in Title 49, U.S.C. Section 40102(a)(15) that further defines the legal meaning "actual control."

S. 1451

Contains no similar provision.

Airline Alliances/Antitrust Exemptions

Several domestic airlines have been partners in the three major international airline alliance groups for many years. United and US Airways, for example, have been part of the "Star Alliance," Continental, Delta, and Northwest have been part of "Skyteam," and American has participated in "Oneworld." Alliances allow partner airlines to jointly market their collective brand internationally, to code share in certain instances, and to otherwise provide air travelers with coordinated services to the many destinations served by each of the partner airlines. In order to participate in an alliance a domestic airline must receive approval, which is essentially an antitrust exemption, from DOT. Over time airlines have changed partner groups. Continental, for example, is currently in the process of moving to the Star Alliance after having received tentative DOT approval for the move in April 2009.

Airlines view these alliances quite favorably and believe they afford each airline with significant competitive advantages. There are other observers, however, who view alliances as being anticompetitive in nature. In this view, the alliance can become a monopoly operator on certain international, especially multinational, routes and can use its market power to preclude new competition, raise fares, and engage in other uncompetitive practices.

---

[56] For a full discussion of airline ownership issues, see CRS Report RL33255, *Legal Developments in International Civil Aviation*, by Todd B. Tatelman.

H.R. 915

House T&I Committee Chairman James Oberstar, as well as other Members of Congress, have long questioned the necessity and/or desirability of alliances for the traveling public. Section 426 of H.R. 915 reflects these concerns and requires that GAO conduct a one-year study of the competitiveness of alliances and the grants of antitrust immunity they receive from DOT. The provision requires that GAO make specific recommendations on the alliance approval process and that the Secretary of Transportation consider these recommendations vis-à-vis possible policy changes to the existing process. The provision sets out certain deadlines for this policy review process. Further, the provision provides for the sunset of all existing alliances three years after enactment of this legislation and requires that future renewal of antitrust immunity not be granted until the Secretary has responded to Congress as to whether and how policy will be changed based on the GAO recommendations.

This provision is of considerable concern to U.S. airlines and to many U.S. trading partners who favor the alliance process. They, and Members of Congress who share their view, see this provision as an unwarranted congressional intrusion into existing international alliance process.

S. 1451

Contains no similar provision.

Airline Passenger Rights Issues

Recent incidents where passengers were held in aircraft for eight or more hours awaiting takeoff, as well as reports of deterioration of on-time arrival performance by airlines, have led to increasing interest in airline passenger consumer issues. Currently, most passenger rights are set forth in the airlines' "contract of carriage" language. The contract of carriage is the legal contract between the airline and the ticket holder which describes the rights and responsibilities of both the air carrier and the passenger. Passengers may take legal action in federal courts based on these contracts. Historically, the Department of Transportation's (DOT) role in consumer protection is limited. The existing law does provide procedures and compensation rules for "bumping" and lost or damaged baggage, however. The main power DOT has to protect consumers is the department's power to take action against air carriers for "deceptive trade practices." The definition and interpretation of deceptive trade practices can significantly impact the scope of DOT's enforcement authority. Staffing of DOT's Office for Aviation Enforcement and Proceedings, however, has been an issue in the past. This DOT office also deals with passenger discrimination issues. Bill section numbers refer to engrossed version H.R. 915 as passed and S. 1451 as introduced.

Airline and Airport "Emergency Contingency Plans" for Tarmac Delays

H.R. 915

The House bill (Section 407) would require, no later than 90 days after the date of enactment, that both air carriers and operators of large or medium hub airports submit to DOT an emergency contingency plan for each of these airports. The plans must describe how the airline plans to provide food, water, restroom facilities, cabin ventilation, and access to medical treatment for passengers on aircraft that are on the ground for extended time without access to the terminal and how they plan to share facilities and make gates available at the airport during an emergency.

Airport operators must also submit an emergency plan describing how the airport operator will provide for the sharing of the use of the airport's facilities and make gates available during an emergency. In the case of airports used for foreign transportation, the airport is to describe how the airport will provide for the use of the terminal to the maximum extent practicable for the processing of passengers arriving at the airport on such flights and in the cases of excessive tarmac delay.

S. 1451

The Senate bill (Section 401) would require that not later than 60 days after the date of enactment, each air carrier and airport operator submit a proposed contingency plan to DOT for review and approval. DOT is to establish minimum standards for these plans to ensure that these plans address long on-board tarmac delays and provide for the health and safety of passengers and crew.

The air carrier plans are to require each air carrier at a minimum to provide essential services, including adequate food, potable water, restroom facilities, cabin ventilation, cabin temperatures, and medical treatment.

Regarding the right to deplane, the plan is to provide passengers with the right to deplane and return to the terminal (when this can be done safely) if: three hours have elapsed since they have boarded and the aircraft doors have been closed; or three hours have elapsed after the aircraft has landed and the passengers have been unable to deplane. The offer to deplane must be repeated at least once every three hours thereafter. Exceptions are allowed if the pilot determines that the aircraft will depart or unload within less than 30 minutes or that permitting a passenger to deplane would jeopardize passenger safety or security. These requirements also apply to diverted flights. After the plan has been reviewed by DOT, it is to be made available to the public. Air carriers must report any flight delayed on the tarmac for over three hours to the Office of Consumer Protection at DOT within 30 days.

The Airport operator must also submit a proposed contingency plan describing how the operator will provide for the deplanement of passengers following a long tarmac delay, will provide for the sharing of facilities, and make gates available for use by aircraft experiencing delays.

Civil penalties may be assessed on any air carrier or airport operator that does not submit, obtain approval of, or adhere to a contingency plan submitted under the bill.

Each air carrier or airport required to submit a contingency plan must ensure public access to the approved plans via their Internet website or by other means determined by DOT.

Advisory Committee for Aviation Consumer Protection

H.R. 915

Section 420 of the House bill requires the Secretary of DOT is to establish an eight-member committee for aviation consumer protection to advise the Secretary in carrying out passenger service improvements.

S. 1451

Section 404 of the Senate bill includes a similar provision, except that the advisory committee would have only four members.

Monthly Air Carrier Reports/Publication of Customer Service data and Flight Delay History

H.R. 915

The bill (Section 402) would require airlines to file monthly reports on flights that are diverted from their scheduled destination to another airport and on flights that depart from the originating airport gate but are cancelled before takeoff. The data must be compiled in a single monthly report and be made available on the DOT website.

S. 1451

Air carriers, on a monthly basis must publish and update on the Internet website of the air carrier, a list of chronically delayed flights operated by the carrier and share the list with each entity that is authorized to book passenger air transportation (e.g., travel agents or websites), for inclusion on the Internet website of the entity.

Air carriers or entities described above must prominently disclose on their Internet websites, at the time of ticket booking, the following: 1) the on-time performance for the flight if the flight is a chronically delayed flight and 2) the cancellation rate for the flight if the flight is a chronically canceled flight. A chronically delayed flight is defined as one that has not been on-time at least 40% of the time in the last three months, and a chronically canceled flight as one whose departures have been canceled at least 30% of the time for the last three months.

Expansion of DOT Airline Consumer Complaint Investigations

H.R. 915

Section 424 requires that, subject to the availability of appropriations, the Secretary of DOT is to investigate consumer complaints regarding: flight cancellations; compliance with federal regulations regarding the overbooking of seats on flights; lost, damaged, or delayed baggage (and problems with air carrier claim procedures); problems with refunds for unused or lost tickets; incorrect or incomplete information on fares, discount fare conditions and availability, overcharges, and fare increases; rights of frequent flier mile holders; and deceptive or misleading advertising. DOT is to provide in an annex to its budget request an estimate of the resources needed to investigate all such claims received by DOT in the previous year.

S. 1451

The Senate bill also includes this provision (Section 403).

Consumer Complaint Hotline Telephone Number

H.R. 915

The House bill (Section 407) would require DOT to establish a consumer complaint hotline telephone number for use by airline passengers. The Secretary of Transportation shall notify the public of the telephone number. Air carriers using aircraft of 30 seats or more shall include on the carrier website, ticket confirmation, or boarding pass issued by the carrier: the hotline number; the email address, telephone number, and mailing address of the air carrier; and the email address, telephone number and mailing address of the Aviation Consumer Protection Division of the Department of Transportation.

S. 1451

The Senate bill (Section 401) also includes a hotline provision. The bill, however, is less prescriptive concerning the means used to publicize the hotline telephone number, simply leaving it up the Secretary of Transportation to publicize the number.

Musical Instruments

H.R. 915

Section 427 of the House bill would require air carriers to permit passengers to stow a musical instrument in the aircraft passenger compartment in a closet, baggage or cargo stowage compartment without charge, if the instrument can be stowed in accordance with the requirements for carriage of carry-on baggage or cargo set forth by the Administrator of the FAA and there is space for such stowage on the aircraft. For instruments too large to be stowed in a closet, baggage or cargo stowage compartment the instrument may be stowed in a seat if it fits and the passenger pays for the seat. An instrument may be treated as checked baggage if the sum of the length, width, and height, including the case does not exceed 150 inches, if its weight does not exceed 165 pounds, and it can be stowed in accordance with the requirements for the stowage of baggage or cargo.

S. 1451

Section 713 of the Senate bill allows passengers to carry small instruments into the cabin of an aircraft as carry-on luggage if the instrument can be stowed in a suitable baggage compartment in the cabin or under a passenger seat and there is space for such stowage at the time the passenger boards the aircraft. Air carriers are to permit a passenger to carry a musical instrument that is too large to meet the above requirements for a small instrument if the instrument is contained in a case, does not exceed 165 pounds in weight (including case), can be secured by a seat belt, does not restrict access to or view of an exit or aisle, does not contain an otherwise illegal object, and the passenger has purchased an additional seat for the instrument. Air carriers are to transport as baggage, without charge, the instrument of a traveling passenger on the flight that may not be carried in the cabin, if the sum of the length, width, and height, including the case does not exceed 150 inches, it weight does not exceed 165 pounds, and it can be stowed in accordance with the requirements for the stowage of baggage or cargo.

Disclosure of Passenger Fees

H.R. 915

The House bill does not include a provision on this issue.

S. 1451

The Senate bill requires the Secretary of Transportation to complete a rulemaking that requires each air carrier operating in the United States to make available to the public and to the Secretary a list of all passenger fees and charges (other than airfare) that may be imposed by the air carrier. The lists are to include fees for: checked baggage or oversized baggage; meals, beverages, or other refreshments; seats in exit rows, seats with additional space, or other preferred seats in any given class of travel; purchasing tickets from an airline ticket agent or travel agency; or any other good, service, or amenity provided by the air carrier, as required by the Secretary. The Secretary may require air carriers to make available the information on their Internet websites, to travel agencies, and in advertising. The secretary shall also require air carriers to update the information as necessary but no less frequently than every 90 days, unless there has been no increase.

DOT Inspector General (IG) Review of Air Carrier Flight Delays, Cancellations, and Associated Causes

H.R. 915

Section 418 of the bill orders the IG to update its 2000 report "Audit of Air Carrier Flight Delays and Cancellations." In conducting the review the IG is directed to assess: 1) the need for an update on delay and cancellation statistics such as chronically delayed flights and taxi-in and taxi-out times; 2) air carrier scheduling practices; 3) the need to reexamine the FAA's airport capacity benchmarks; 4) the impact of flight delays and cancellations on passengers and recommendations to address these impacts; and 5) the effect that limited air carrier service options on routes have on the frequency of delays and cancellations on such routes.

S. 1451

The Senate bill does not include this provision.

Notification of Flight Status by Text Message or Email

H.R. 915

Section 407 requires the Secretary of Transportation, within 180 days, to issue regulations to require air carriers having 1% of the total domestic scheduled-service passenger revenue to provide each passenger an option to receive a text message, email or other comparable electronic service, subject to any fees applicable under the contract of the passenger for the electronic service, with notification of any change in the status of the flight before the boarding process begins.

S. 1451

The Senate bill does not include this provision.

Denied Boarding Compensation

H.R. 915

Section 421 requires that, not later than May 19, 2010, and every two years thereafter, the Secretary of DOT shall evaluate the amount provided for denied-boarding compensation and issue a regulation to adjust such compensation as necessary.

S. 1451

The Senate bill does not include this provision.

Delayed Baggage Compensation

H.R. 915

Section 422 requires GAO to conduct a study to 1) examine delays in the delivery of checked baggage to passengers and 2) make recommendations for establishing minimum standards to compensate passengers in the case of unreasonable delays in checked baggage delivery.

GAO is to consider the additional fees for checked baggage that are now imposed by some air carriers and how the additional fees should improve an air carrier's baggage performance. Results are to be reported 180 days after enactment.

S. 1451

The Senate bill does not include this provision.

Study of European Union Rules for Passenger Rights

H.R. 915

Section 419 requires GAO to conduct a study to evaluate and compare the regulations of the European Union and the United States on compensation offered to passengers who are denied boarding or whose flights are cancelled or delayed.

S. 1451

The Senate bill does not include this provision.

Insecticide Use on Passenger Aircraft

H.R. 915

Section 407 requires the Secretary of Transportation to establish a public Internet website that lists countries that may require an air carrier to treat an aircraft passenger cabin with insecticides. Air carriers or ticket agents selling tickets in the United States for a foreign destination listed in the DOT website shall disclose on their own website or through other means that the destination country may require the carrier to treat the cabin with insecticides.

S. 1451

The Senate bill does not include this provision.

Prohibitions Against Cell Phone or Other Voice Communication Devices

H.R. 915

The bill would prohibit use by an individual, other than members of the flight crews or federal law enforcement officers, of a mobile communications device in an aircraft during a flight in scheduled passenger interstate or intrastate air transportation. "Voice communications using a mobile communications device" includes a commercial mobile radio service or other wireless communications device; a broadband wireless device or other wireless device that transmits data packets using the Internet Protocol or comparable technical standard; or a device having voice override capability.

S. 1451

The Senate bill does not include this provision.

Airport Master Plans

H.R. 915

In Section 153 of the bill, the Secretary of Transportation is to encourage airport sponsors and state and local officials to consider customer convenience, airport ground access, and access to airport facilities in airport master plans.

S. 1451

The Senate bill does not include this provision.

Smoking Prohibition

H.R. 915

Section 401 amends the smoking prohibition set forth in 49 U.S.C. 41707. It clarifies that the prohibition applies to passenger flights, both international and domestic. It also broadens the coverage to include nonscheduled intrastate, interstate, or international flights if a flight attendant is a required crewmember of the aircraft.

S. 1451

The Senate bill does not include this provision.

Study of Air Cleaning Technology

H.R. 915

The House bill does not include a provision on this issue.

S. 1451

Section 613, added to the introduced version of the bill during mark-up by the Committee on Commerce, Science, and Transportation, requires a new FAA research program be established for air cleaning technology, including research of sensor technology for engine and passenger unit bleed air (regarding aircraft cabin air quality).

Author Contact Information

Bart Elias, Coordinator
Specialist in Aviation Policy
belias@crs.loc.gov, 7-7771

John W. Fischer
Specialist in Transportation Policy
jfischer@crs.loc.gov, 7-7766

Robert S. Kirk
Specialist in Transportation Policy
rkirk@crs.loc.gov, 7-7769

Linda Luther
Analyst in Environmental Policy
lluther@crs.loc.gov, 7-6852

Carol Hardy Vincent
Specialist in Natural Resources Policy
chvincent@crs.loc.gov, 7-8651

Brent D. Yacobucci
Specialist in Energy and Environmental Policy
byacobucci@crs.loc.gov, 7-9662

James E. McCarthy
Specialist in Environmental Policy
jmccarthy@crs.loc.gov, 7-7225

Jon O. Shimabukuro
Legislative Attorney
jshimabukuro@crs.loc.gov, 7-7990

Todd B. Tatelman
Legislative Attorney
ttatelman@crs.loc.gov, 7-4697

Key CRS Policy Staff and Areas of Expertise

The table below provides a quick reference for congressional staff seeking to identify experts to contact regarding specific issues or aspects of FAA Reauthorization legislation.

Table 4. Contact Information for CRS Policy Staff

Name	Areas of Expertise	Division	Telephone
Bart Elias	—Next Generation Air Traffic System (NGATS)	RSI	7-7771
	—FAA Facilities and Equipment (F&E)		
	—FAA Management and Operations		
	—Airport and Airspace Demand and Capacity Analysis		
	—Aviation Safety		
	—Aircraft Noise Policy and Quiet Aircraft Technology		
John Fischer	—FAA Financing and Aviation Taxes	RSI	7-7766
	—Airport and Airways Trust Fund (AATF)		
	—Essential Air Service and Small Community Air Service Development Programs		
	—Airline Economic Issues		
Bob Kirk	—FAA Financing and Aviation Taxes	RSI	7-7769
	—Airport and Airways Trust Fund (AATF)		
	—Airport Improvement Program (AIP)		
	—Airport Finance		
Linda Luther	—Airport Environmental Issues	RSI	7-6852
Carol Hardy Vincent	—Air Tour Management Program	RSI	7-8651
	—Aviation Impacts on National Parks		
Jim McCarthy	—Aircraft Emissions	RSI	7-7225
Brent Yacobucci	—Aviation Fuels	RSI	7-9662
	—Alternative Fuels for Aircraft and Ground Support Vehicles		
Jon Shimabukuro	—Labor Law and Policy	ALD	7-7990
	—FAA Labor Relations		
Todd Tatelman	—Aviation Law (Domestic and International)	ALD	7-4697

www.ingramcontent.com/pod-product-compliance
Lightning Source LLC
Chambersburg PA
CBHW052009280526
45793CB00005B/904